ALL MY

BONES

SHAKE

ALL MY

BONES

SHAKE

SEEKING A PROGRESSIVE PATH

TO THE PROPHETIC VOICE

ROBERT

JENSEN

Soft Skull Press

Brooklyn

Library of Congress Cataloging-in-Publication Data is available.
ISBN: 978-1-59376-234-6

Cover design by Brett Yasko
Interior design by Neuwirth & Associates, Inc.
Printed in the United States of America

Soft Skull Press
An Imprint of Counterpoint LLC
1919 Fifth Street
Berkeley, CA 94710
www.softskull.com
www.counterpointpress.com
Distributed by Publishers Group West

10 9 8 7 6 5 4 3

Concerning the prophets:
My heart is broken within me,
all my bones shake;
I am like a drunken man,
like a man overcome by wine,
because of the LORD
and because of his holy words.

[JER. 23:9]

CONTENTS

ACKNOWLEDGMENTS

Although I am listed as the sole author, this is more of a collaborative effort than any of my previous books. The primary uncredited coauthors are James Koplin, Eliza Gilkyson, and Jim Rigby. My relationship with each one has changed me in profound ways, and significant parts of this book are the direct result of my conversations with them. Each knows what this means and how deeply their influence on me runs. To each I owe debts that can only be repaid with the promise of love and loyalty.

Many others have helped me along the way through conversation and collective action, including Junaid Ahmad, Gene Burd, Bob Dailey, Farid Esack, Abe Osheroff, Carlos Perez de Alejo, Diane Rhodes, Sean Tate, Pat Youngblood, and Zbigniew Zabinski. Thanks to Charles Spencer for more than two decades of work as my most consistent and critical editor, and to Pam Wagner for her thoughtful reading and careful editing.

We are also sometimes deeply affected by people we never meet but know through their writing. The work of many such people is woven through this book, but none more profound than that of Wes Jackson, cofounder of the Land Institute. Jackson is typically identified as a leader in research on sustainable agriculture, which is true enough. But his contributions go far beyond that specific field, and his writings and lectures have been a rich source of insight for me.[1]

---

1 Information about the Land Institute is online at http://www.landinstitute.org/. Jackson's books include *Becoming Native to this Place* (Washington D.C.: Counterpoint, 1996), *Altars of Unhewn Stone: Science and the Earth* (San Francisco: North Point Press, 1987), and *New Roots for Agriculture* (Lincoln: University of Nebraska Press, 1980). A video of Jackson's presentation "The Next 50 Years on the American Land" at the 2008 Chautauqua Institution program is online at http://fora.tv/2008/08/15/Wes_Jackson_The_Next_50_Years_on_the_American_Land.

PREFACE

I am a professor, but this is not a scholarly work. I am a church member, but this is not a proselytizing tract. I emphasize these things not only in the interest of intellectual honesty but also in the hope it will increase people's interest in reading. I assume, first, that readers who have suffered through the turgid prose of most academic texts are reluctant to pick up a book that offers more of the same; and, second, that readers who have suffered through others' attempts to convert them will avoid anything that appears aimed at revealing the truth to the uninitiated.

This book is my attempt to make sense of the struggle over the meaning of Christianity for those of us living in the contemporary United States. Given the dominance of Christianity in this country and the dominance, albeit fading, of the United States in the world, anyone concerned about the future of the planet should be concerned about that struggle. People from other societies and other faith traditions may find what I say relevant, but I am aware of the limits of my inquiry. I impose them on myself not because of a lack of interest in other places and their religions, but because of my obligations as a privileged citizen of the empire. I take my primary task to be to come to terms with the dominant theology and politics of the United States as I engage in the continuing struggle for social justice and ecological sustainability.

So this is an exercise in lay theology in an explicitly political context, aimed at grappling with the questions of the ages in the context of contemporary crises. Readers of theologians such as Marcus Borg and John Dominic Crossan will find some familiar themes here, as will readers of political and cultural analysts such as Noam Chomsky, Andrea Dworkin, and Wendell Berry.[2] Readers also may find all these ideas integrated in ways that are unfamiliar. If this book is of value, it will likely be because I have written as honestly as I can, in plain language, about my struggles to come to terms with these theological questions in the context of the politics that I think necessary to imagine a decent future. I do not claim to be an expert in the field of theology, which to some may limit the scope or value of my insights. On the other hand, I'm not burdened by claims of expertise, which may well be to my advantage.

A note on biblical references: In preparing this book I used the Revised Standard version of the Bible, mostly for sentimental reasons. I received a copy at the First Presbyterian Church of Fargo, North Dakota, when I was in the third grade. I still have that Bible, which still has my name on the front in gold letters. The photograph on the cover of this book—an eight-year-old Robert Jensen holding that Bible—was taken after that church service in May 1967.

---

2 For examples of their work, see Marcus J. Borg, *Reading the Bible Again for the First Time: Taking the Bible Seriously but Not Literally* (New York: HarperCollins, 2001); John Dominic Crossan, *Jesus: A Revolutionary Biography* (New York: HarperCollins, 1995); Noam Chomsky, *The Essential Chomsky* (New York: New Press, 2008); Andrea Dworkin, *Letters from a War Zone* (Chicago: Lawrence Hill Books, 1993); and Wendell Berry, *What Are People For?* (San Francisco: North Point Press, 1990).

ALL MY

BONES

SHAKE

INTRODUCTION

Political Theology,
Theological Politics

Perhaps one of the few human universals is a shared sense of awe at the scale and scope of the universe and at the complexity and diversity of life on this planet. The capacity to experience that awe—which inspires and confounds scientists and artists, as well as us ordinary folks, secular and religious alike—may be what marks us as human. Sadly, almost as common is the human tendency toward a smug sense of certainty in our own answers to the questions that arise out of that awe.

For an example of that, take a look at the 2006 British documentary *The Root of All Evil?* in which biologist Richard Dawkins critiques religion and religious faith.[3] In Part I of the film, Dawkins travels to the evangelical Christian New Life Church in Colorado Springs, Colorado, to observe a service and interview Ted Haggard, the founder and then pastor of the church (who later that year resigned in a sex-and-drug scandal).

---

3 Channel 4 (UK), *The Root of All Evil?*: Episode 1, "The God Delusion"; Episode 2, "The Virus of Faith." http://www.channel4.com/culture/microsites/C/can_you_believe_it/debates/rootofevil.html

Dawkins and Haggard accuse each other of being unwilling to consider opposing views. When Haggard makes an incorrect assertion about evolutionary theory that reveals his lack of scientific knowledge, Dawkins concludes, "You obviously know nothing about the subject of evolution." Haggard suggests that Dawkins's "intellectual arrogance" limits his ability to talk to people of faith. Both conclusions seem reasonable. Dawkins is right to point out that Haggard doesn't seem to understand basic biology and doesn't seem to care, and Haggard is right to point out that Dawkins is haughty and doesn't seem to care. But neither man appears to be trying to get beyond caricaturing the other man, which means viewers learn little from the encounter. What if Dawkins had been truly curious about what leads the members of Haggard's congregation to such strong faith? What if Haggard had realized he could learn something from a top-flight biologist? What is lost when we stay stuck in caricatures?

Such is our fate these days: We live in a world awash in debate about religion, spirituality, and faith that often seems to derail rather than deepen our quest to understand the world in which we struggle to live fully and responsibly. The problem is not the clashing of ideas; such clashes often advance knowledge. Nor is the problem that such debates can be on occasion sharp-edged and tense; such edginess is common, maybe inevitable, when people disagree about important issues. The problem is simply that the conflict is rarely constructive.

When evangelical minister Rick Warren and atheist Sam Harris squared off for *Newsweek*, the conversation didn't produce much that deepened my understanding of the issues. Warren accused atheists of being intolerant of Christians. Harris rejected that claim and argued that religion is the one type of "divisive dogmatism."

WARREN: You don't feel atheists are dogmatic?

HARRIS: No, I don't.

WARREN: I'm sorry, I disagree with you. You're quite dogmatic.

HARRIS: OK, well, I'm happy to have you point out my dogmas, but first . . ."[4]

And so it goes, as this debate in the United States that pits fundamentalist believers against fundamentalist atheists routinely falls into the intellectual equivalent of schoolyard taunting:

There is a God.
No there isn't.
You can't prove there isn't.
You can't prove there is.

Off to the side of this titanic clash are the theological moderates and the undeclared agnostics, whose most common strategy seems to be to avoid being drawn into defending a clear position, hoping that a kind of mushy tolerance—"Can't we all just get along?" in regard to disputes over the ultimate questions—can substitute for more substantive answers.

So we have forthright fundamentalists (religious and secular) eager to draw lines in the sand, along with receding relativists (religious and secular) happy to bury their heads in the same sand. Meanwhile, there are lots of people looking for other ways to engage these questions, people who find the answers from all these camps to be inadequate in the struggle to build a livable world in which humans might survive humanely into another

---

4 "God Debate: Sam Harris vs. Rick Warren," *Newsweek*, April 9, 2007. http://www.msnbc.msn.com/id/17889148/site/newsweek/print/1/displaymode/1098/

century. I am one of those, searching not for a way to resolve those debates but to transcend the gridlock. Luckily, we aren't confined to the four positions in that matrix. We can ponder the reasons for the origins of religions, examine centuries of struggle over their meaning, and incorporate secular philosophy and history to fashion a spirituality that can help us come to terms with our world. Such a spirituality is desperately needed as we face stark choices about how to cope with a world organized around profoundly unjust and fundamentally unsustainable systems (capitalism within nation-states with their roots in patriarchy and white-supremacy), which leave us facing cascading crises—political and economic, cultural and spiritual, and most important, ecological.

At this historical moment, the stakes are high, and in the coming years our choices on all those fronts are likely to have permanent consequences, not just for our future but for the fate of the planet. Every serious study of the state of the ecosystem indicates we have, at best, a few decades to come to terms with these crises. The most recent *Living Planet Report* notes that humanity's demands on resources exceed the planet's regenerative capacity by about 30 percent. "If we continue with business as usual, by the early 2030s we will need two planets to keep up with humanity's demand for goods and services," the report concludes.[5]

To imagine a just and sustainable world, we need not just a politics but also a theology that can help us face the delusional arrogance and disastrous self-indulgence of humans, especially humans of the modern industrial era. These qualities have put us on a collision course with natural forces more powerful than we

---

5 *Living Planet Report 2008*, World Wildlife Fund for Nature, October 2008, p. 3. http://assets.panda.org/downloads/living_planet_report_2008.pdf

can ever hope to understand fully or control much at all. There's a chance—with no guarantee, of course—that we can draw on the best of our traditions and find the strength within ourselves that will be required to alter that course and create a world that is both just and sustainable. If we cannot create such a world, we will need that deepest strength to cope with the grim realities we will face in a future that we cannot now imagine.[6]

These are the end times, of a sort. I am not talking about rapture and tribulation, but about rupture and triangulation. The challenge isn't to anticipate the return of Christ but to face the reality that we modern humans have created unsustainable social and ecological systems that have ruptured the world, and we need the insights of all our best traditions to triangulate from multiple viewpoints and devise new ways to live. We are facing the end of an era of irresponsible human domination of the planet, which cannot—and will not—continue much longer. I do not fear the apocalypse as it is imagined by end-time Christians (a dramatic finish with the saved being lifted up and the damned left behind in a heap of trouble) but rather a steady erosion of the conditions that make possible a minimally decent human existence in the context of respect for other forms of life.

With those realities, threats, and challenges in mind, I offer the following thesis:

There is no God, and more than ever we all need to serve the One True Gods.

This book is an attempt to make sense of that apparently

---

6 For visions of such a grim future, see Cormac McCarthy, *The Road* (New York: Vintage, 2006) and Octavia Butler, *The Parable of the Sower* (New York: Four Walls Eight Windows, 1993) and *The Parable of the Talents* (New York: Seven Stories, 1998).

nonsensical sentence with its deliberate singular/plural confusion, to which I'll return in the concluding chapter. But for now, my task in proposing this idea to those who are religious is to defend vigorously the first clause in the sentence, the assertion that "there is no God." That task wouldn't be quite so difficult if we would keep reminding ourselves of one simple reality:

Humans created religion; religion did not create humans.

Whatever one believes about the nature of the divine, it clearly was humans who developed the doctrines and ceremonies to express spirituality. That means we can change and update those traditions as we learn more about ourselves and the world around us.

To those who are secular, the second clause—the assertion that "we all need to serve the One True Gods"—needs considerable explanation. But the statement wouldn't seem so obscure if we could keep reminding ourselves of another fundamental reality:

Inanimate matter created life; life did not create inanimate matter.

At a point when human activity is threatening to undermine the capacity of the ecosystem to sustain human life as we know it, it's crucial that we keep our arrogance in check and remember that we are not a creator but instead a part of Creation.

Taken together, these two simple reminders suggest that when we look to the spiritual realm and religion for insights into how we should live in this world, we must remember that religion is our creation. Likewise, when we look to the secular realm and science for insights into how the world works, we must remember our place in Creation.

I want to articulate a conception of theology, and argue for its importance, in a way that may provoke some folks on all sides—religious fundamentalists and relativists, as well as secular fundamentalists and relativists. Although I have a deep contrarian streak in me, that instinct is not the motive force here. I have spent most of my fifty years studiously ignoring theological debates, which seemed annoying and irrelevant. I still often find them annoying, but I no longer feel I have the luxury of opting out of theological conversations. After a period of listening to the conversations of others, I have concluded that two important things must happen if we are to move forward. Stated provocatively, by design:

To the fundamentalists on both sides: Grow up.
To the moderates on both sides: Buck up.

Both religious and secular fundamentalists tend to be convinced that they *really* know what they claim to know, which makes them unrealistically confident in their judgments based on those knowledge claims. These are childlike claims; respectfully, I will argue that people who make them need to grow up.

Moderates, both religious and secular, typically are less insistent about the absolute truth of what they claim to know, and as a result often are hesitant to judge. These are irresponsible positions; respectfully, I will argue that people who take them need to buck up.

Although these two "requests" are formulated in what could be seen as harsh language ("grow up" and "buck up" typically are instructions to the immature and the weak-willed) they are not meant that way. It is not difficult to understand why so many people seek certainty in a complex and confusing world, nor is it hard to understand the desire to avoid making judgments about others when one is aware of the limits of one's own knowledge. The crucial work of theology today is to help us abandon any pretense of secure knowledge, but at the same time provide the confidence and courage to judge—and act on those judgments—despite the inevitable risks that come with human limits.

It's time to face questions for which we have no answers, to address problems for which there may be no solutions. We have to accept the radical uncertainty of our lives, yet meet the challenges that life puts in front of us. To help us cope, what kind of theology—what ideas about what it means to be a human being at this moment in time—will we need?

CHRISTIAN IDEAS

In a world with no settled answer to the question "What does it mean to be a Christian?" anyone claiming that identity has to find his or her own answer, whether it comes straight out of traditional teaching or from a personal struggle and synthesis. Typically, people ask: "What do Christians believe?" I begin with a slightly different question: "What is the animating spirit at the heart of Christianity?" One way I think through that is by asking a slightly less formal question: "What kind of Christians do I want to be around?"

The Christians I find myself drawn to are those who seek deeper insight into the aspects of the world that are beyond our capacity to understand fully; flourish in community with others; demonstrate a principled commitment to social justice and ecological sustainability; operate in the context of a dynamic, not static, faith; and are aware that our particular spiritual route is one of many principled paths, not the only possibility. In world history, there have been many such seekers, some religious and some secular. One mark of these people is their willingness to cross boundaries to speak with each other. But in Christianity, and many other religions, there has always been a segment of the faithful who accept a locked-down or locked-in conception of the faith, one that is narrow and rigid, focused on rituals and doctrine rather than community and struggle. Those are the Christians I find it less rewarding to be around.

My hope for this book is that those engaged in struggles similar to mine will find my experience and ideas helpful, while those who find comfort in a more rigid interpretation might consider the alternatives. I would make the same pitch to Muslims, Jews, Hindus, Buddhists, and those of other faiths or no faith—for all who share a common sense of self, others, and the larger world. In those traditions, people pursuing a more expansive conception of faith often face similar challenges. Just as I have learned from their work, I hope my struggles are of value to them.[7]

History suggests that many of the earliest Christians shared some of the beliefs of today's theological progressives but that those views unfortunately lost out over time to more authoritarian forces imposing rigid doctrinal conceptions of faith. But history is elusive, and whatever the reality of any religion's origins, our task today is not to return to some imagined past but to claim the best of older traditions in light of the demands placed on us by the contemporary world.

One aspect of that pressing reality today is the greatly expanded scale of our lives, which now play out on a global scale. We live rooted in specific places with specific people, yet we have to see beyond. We humans—all of us, no matter where

---

7 I am particularly indebted to Farid Esack, *On Being a Muslim: Finding a Religious Path in the World Today* (Oxford, UK: Oneworld, 1999) and *Qur'an, Liberation and Pluralism: An Islamic Perspective on Interreligious Solidarity against Oppression* (Oxford, UK: Oneworld, 1997).

we live today—are fundamentally tribal people, yet history's trajectory has made us one global people, interdependent in ways that cannot be disentangled. We live in local communities, with moral and material connections to the entire planet. We are particular and universal. This is especially true of those of us living with privilege in the first world, for the wealth on which we float so comfortably was largely extracted from the third world, a fact that creates obligations we cannot ignore if we want to continue to claim to believe in the principles we articulate. I'll return to this in more detail in the conclusion.

The willingness to adapt the best aspects of specific traditions to face the demands of the universal present is crucial if one is to accept the ultimate, if somewhat paradoxical, goal for Christians: We should search the faith for a way to transcend the faith. The wisdom in Christianity has much to contribute, along with the wisdom of other faiths and secular philosophy. So we can take seriously Christianity today in the hope that someday it will give way to a new synthesis, an integration of the best of all the spiritual and secular traditions in a truly universal understanding, mediated through the local stories that people find compelling to tell and retell. We can seek a Christianity that we hope can one day merge into what would be called simply a deeper collective humanity. It is a futile task, of course, one that can never be achieved fully and maybe will never be achieved in any sense. But it is our task, one worth undertaking.

And what would this Christianity help us understand? Historically, religions have addressed three key questions:

How did the world come to be?
What is our fate after death?
How shall we live while we are here?

The first two questions are intriguing but, ultimately, not of great concern to me. To the degree we can know anything about the first question, answers will come from science, though the answers always will be incomplete. We know that we are but one species on one planet around one star that exists in a galaxy with billions of other stars, itself one of billions of galaxies. At the same time, we also know that each of us has within our own bodies billions of cells that interact in ways so complex we cannot hope ever to understand ourselves fully. In short, it's a big big world out there, and a big small world inside us, and we should accept that our understanding of these things is always bound to be limited. That's why origin myths are common to all cultures, including those dominated by science. Exploring this question through stories acknowledges that no matter what the scientific advances, there is no final scientific answer to that one.

As for the second question, I cannot imagine how humans can do much more than speculate about our fate after death. I know that many people spend a considerable amount of time pondering this one, but it's not a particularly intriguing question for me. I don't mean that I can't see why it is an interesting question to many, nor would I contend that I laugh in the face of death or can comfortably predict that when death comes round my door I will be without fear. I expect when that happens, I will react like most people—confused and scared. But I do know I have never thought that the question of what will happen to me after I die was important enough to fuss much about while I'm trying to get on with the business of living.

My relative lack of interest in those questions—not just today, but from my earliest childhood memories—has left me free to concentrate on the third question, which is the one that I believe matters the most. What is the nature of our obligations to ourselves, to others, and to the nonhuman world? Given our answers to those questions, which political projects are most important? Anyone concerned with such questions cannot avoid the political—the struggle to understand how power operates and the obligation to intervene in the world to try to create a more just and sustainable society. But in addition to politics, there is more.

THEOLOGY POLITICALLY

My first venture into political activism was gender politics. When I first started giving talks critiquing men's violence against women and men's use of women in the sexual-exploitation industries (stripping, pornography, prostitution), I searched for ways to highlight not just the consequences of these destructive activities but the underlying conception of what it means to be a man that most of us have been socialized to accept: masculinity expressed as a quest for control and domination, routinely leading to aggression and violence. Our understanding of what it means to be male has to change, I argued. To drive home that point, I often ended talks with a challenge to my brothers:

You can be a man, or you can be a human being.

The point was not that we men should alter our bodies but that we should rethink this component of our identity. I was suggesting that we couldn't retain a loyalty to masculinity and still live fully human lives. I later adapted that question for talks on racism, United States foreign policy, and economics. We can be white people, or we can be human beings. We can be Americans, or we can be human beings. We can be affluent, or we can be human beings.

The common claim is simple: To embrace being a man in the conventional sense is to accept the oppression of women in patriarchy; to embrace being a white person in a racist society is to accept the oppression of nonwhite people; to embrace being American in a world dominated by our hyperviolent nation-state is to accept profound injustice in the world; and to embrace being affluent in a world structured by predatory corporate capitalism is to accept the deprivation that billions around the world endure.

Underneath those claims is a structural analysis of the roots of an unjust and unsustainable system and a conclusion that for all its affluence and military power, the United States is in many ways a society in collapse. On all fronts—politically, economically, culturally, and most important, ecologically—we are in trouble. We live in an increasingly callous culture that exploits sexuality and glorifies violence, often with racist images and themes; embedded in a house-of-cards economy built on orgiastic consumption, deepening personal and collective debt, and an artificially inflated dollar; at the end of an imperial era that is grinding to a potentially disastrous demise. And as if that weren't enough, looming behind all those crises are the consequences of ignoring for too long the unraveling ecological fabric that makes life possible.

This framework no doubt would seem radical, even crazy, to many United States citizens. It indeed is radical, in the foundational sense of the term: going to the root, trying to understand the nature of things. Radical analyses go below the surface to look at the underlying systems and structures of power. In this new century, we need radical analyses more than ever. That's not crazy, but is in fact the only sane response to a world facing such crises. Radical is realistic, and realistic is sane.

When we dare to be radical, we confront the reality that, at both the personal and planetary levels, we are surrounded by systems based on a domination/subordination dynamic, which we have to challenge at all levels. It's important to be clear about these particular systems—race, gender and sexuality, capitalism, and empire—all of which must be examined in the context of the coming ecological collapse.

A focus on the first two, race and gender, is often dismissed as mere "identity politics," and there is certainly a way in which a shallow "diversity talk" can derail radical politics. But there is no way to talk about progressive social change in this country and the wider world if we don't confront the pathologies of white supremacy and patriarchy, both of which are woven deeply into the fabric of this society. Such terms may seem old-fashioned, but we live in a world of enduring racialized disparities in wealth and well-being, rooted not in the inadequacy of people of color but in white dominance,[8] and a world in which women still face the social limitations and physical threats that come from male dominance.[9]

We also can see that those ideologies of white supremacy and patriarchy are linked to the systems of capitalism and empire, which are rooted in the glorification of a hypercompetitive, violent masculinity and in a belief in the inherent superiority of the United States and Europe. Capitalism creates a world defined by greed and attempts to reduce us to crass maximizers of self-interest—not exactly a recipe for living a decent life consistent with our moral and/or theological principles. Empire allows the extraction of the wealth of the many to enrich an ever-smaller

---

8 Robert Jensen, *The Heart of Whiteness: Confronting Race, Racism, and White Privilege* (San Francisco: City Lights Books, 2005).

9 Robert Jensen, *Getting Off: Pornography and the End of Masculinity* (Cambridge: South End Press, 2007).

number of people, not exactly a morally and/or theologically defensible model.[10]

These systems leave a third of the people on the planet to live on less than $2 per day, while half live on less than $2.50 a day.[11] Let that statistic sink in: More than 3 billion people survive—struggling for food, shelter, clothing, education, medical care—on less than what one of us in the developed world might spend on a fancy cup of coffee in the morning. The people living at that level of poverty are disproportionately nonwhite and female. They live mostly in a third world that has suffered, and continues to suffer, from military and/or economic domination by the first world, especially today by the United States. Radical politics says not only that this state of affairs is unjust, but that the systems and structures of power that give rise to it are fundamentally unjust and must be changed.

And then there is the question of sustainability. While public awareness of the depth of the ecological crisis is growing, our knowledge of the basics of the problem is hardly new. For example, in 1992, about 1,700 of the world's leading scientists issued a warning, which began:

> Human beings and the natural world are on a collision course. Human activities inflict harsh and often irreversible damage on the environment and on critical resources. If not checked, many of our current practices put at serious risk the future that we wish for human society and the plant and animal kingdoms, and may so alter the living world that it will be unable to sustain life in the

---

10 Robert Jensen, *Citizens of the Empire: The Struggle to Claim Our Humanity* (San Francisco: City Lights Books, 2004).

11 World Bank, *World Development Report 2008*, October 2007. www.worldbank.org/wdr2008

manner that we know. Fundamental changes are urgent if we are to avoid the collision our present course will bring about.[12]

Look at any crucial measure of the health of the ecosphere in which we live—groundwater depletion, topsoil loss, chemical contamination, increased toxicity in our own bodies, the number and size of "dead zones" in the oceans, accelerating extinction of species and reduction of biodiversity—and ask a simple question: Where we are heading?[13] Remember also that we live in an oil-based world that is fast running out of oil, which means we face a huge reconfiguration of the infrastructure that undergirds our lives.[14] And, of course, there is the undeniable trajectory of rapid climate change.[15]

Add all that up, and it's not a pretty picture. It's crucial that we realize there are no technological fixes that will rescue us. We have to go to the root and acknowledge that human attempts to dominate the nonhuman world have failed. We are destroying the planet and in the process destroying ourselves. Here, just as in human relationships, we either abandon the domination/subordination dynamic or we don't survive.

A radically realistic assessment of the nature of contemporary

---

12 Henry Kendall, a Nobel Prize physicist and former chair of the Union of Concerned Scientists' board of directors, was the primary author of the "World Scientists' Warning to Humanity." http://www.ucsusa.org/ucs/about/1992-world-scientists.html

13 For an assessment, see Lester R. Brown, *Plan B 3.0: Mobilizing to Save Civilization*, 3rd ed. (New York: W. W. Norton, 2008).

14 For an accessible review of the data and a blunt evaluation of options, see James Howard Kunstler, *The Long Emergency: Surviving the End of Oil, Climate Change, and Other Converging Catastrophes of the Twenty-First Century* (New York: Grove, 2006).

15 For a clear summary of that issue, see Fred Pearce, *With Speed and Violence: Why Scientists Fear Tipping Points in Climate Change* (Boston: Beacon, 2007).

systems and institutions is necessary if we are to make progress toward real justice and real sustainability. It is realistic, though not pleasant to recognize, that when we draw our sense of self from the privilege and power that comes with being in a dominant position within unjust and immoral hierarchical systems— patriarchy, white supremacy, United States imperial domination, and capitalism—we sacrifice some deeper sense of our humanity. We can't accept those privileges and that power without losing a part of ourselves, the part that gives real meaning to our lives, the part with which we yearn to connect to others.

You can be a man, or you can be a human being.
You can be white, or you can be a human being.
You can be an American, or you can be a human being.
You can be affluent, or you can be a human being.

Those choices clarify and confront. They ask us to consider our positions in systems, to assess our role in institutions, to ponder our complicity with injustice, to go beyond the comforting clichés of American triumphalism.

But when I posed these choices in political talks and writings, I always left one obvious question unasked and unanswered: What does it mean to be a human being? That is, given all that we know and don't know in the modern world, what does a claim to be human really mean at this moment in history? What qualities are we most focused on when we say we are human, when we talk about our humanity? We appeal to each other's humanity all the time, but with surprisingly little discussion of what it means in the modern context.

As I worked on political issues connected to these systems of oppression—patriarchy, white supremacy, United States empire, capitalism, human domination—I found that the political traditions in which I was rooted gave me the tools I needed to analyze and resist those systems. Radical feminism, antiracist theory and practice, traditional anti-imperialist and anticapitalist movements, and the best thinking in ecology—all were more than adequate for providing an understanding of how these systems work and for putting together a holistic analysis of a profoundly unjust and immoral modern world. Political analysis took me a long way toward where I wanted to be.

But increasingly I had a sense those traditions could not take me all the way home. I had difficulty fashioning an answer to that nagging question: What does it mean to be human?

POLITICS THEOLOGICALLY

So it was then, somewhat reluctantly, that I turned to theology and eventually joined a congregation. My motivation wasn't a sudden surge of interest in the origins of the universe or a concern about what awaited me after death; my focus remained on the question of how to live fully and responsibly in the here and now. The same questions that had led me to progressive politics nudged me to expand the scope of my inquiry. I had no interest in succumbing to New Age–style self-indulgence, nor did I intend to give up politics to pursue theology. My goal has been to deepen my politics through theology and to open up to new ways of thinking about myself as well. Whatever I had thought of religious institutions in the past—I had never cared much for them—increasingly it seemed self-defeating to avoid engagement with religion, which is so clearly a powerful force for so many.

When I put all this together—my political experience and emerging theological inquiries, in the context of the multiple crises we face—I searched for language for my struggles. The first step was not to answer questions but to pose questions clearly, in ways that would allow people of different views at least to start from some common ground. If I were to condense all this into one question, it would look like this:

Which practices, systems, and fundamental conceptions of what it means to be human are consistent with a sustainable human presence on the earth, respectful of other life, in societies that provide the necessary resources for all people to live a decent life, within a culture that fosters individual flourishing alongside a meaningful sense of collective identity, helping us to take seriously our obligations to ourselves, each other, and to the non-human world?

Embedded in that one question are, of course, many complex questions. In this book I do not pretend to answer them so much as think through an approach to facing the questions. For a framework, I draw on an often-quoted part of Mark's Gospel:[16]

---

16 There also are versions of this in Luke and Matthew.

[25] And behold, a lawyer stood up to put him to the test, saying, "Teacher, what shall I do to inherit eternal life?" [26] He said to him, "What is written in the law? How do you read?" [27] And he answered, "You shall love the Lord your God with all your heart, and with all your soul, and with all your strength, and with all your mind; and your neighbor as yourself." [LUKE 10:25-27]

[35] And one of them, a lawyer, asked him a question, to test him. [36] "Teacher, which is the great commandment in the law?" [37] And he said to him, "You shall love the Lord your God with all your heart, and with all your soul, and with all your mind. [38] This is the great and first commandment. [39] And a second is like it, You shall love your neighbor as yourself." [MATT. 22:35-39]

As well as in the Old Testament.

[4] "Hear, O Israel: The LORD our God is one LORD; [5] and you shall love the LORD your God with all your heart, and with all your soul, and with all your might. [DEUT. 6:4-5]

[28] And one of the scribes came up and heard them disputing with one another, and seeing that he answered them well, asked him, "Which commandment is the first of all?" [29] Jesus answered, "The first is, 'Hear, O Israel: The Lord our God, the Lord is one; [30] and you shall love the Lord your God with all your heart, and with all your soul, and with all your mind, and with all your strength.' [31] The second is this, 'You shall love your neighbor as yourself.' There is no other commandment greater than these."

[MARK 12:28–31]

Israel was a particular community, but Jesus reminded people that they were part of the universal, of the single God, the same God who presided over the larger human community. How do we make sense of that struggle to live with our tribal roots yet be part of the world? How do we all, as tribal people, live out that universal? It certainly will take all of our heart, soul, mind, and strength to struggle to know the truth and then act on it, to love our neighbors—defined not literally as those living close to us, but as all the world's people—as if they were of our particular tribe.

Slightly reordered—starting with mind and moving next to heart, then soul and strength—that "first of all" the commandments forms the structure for my exploration and the arguments of this book. Like any scheme for dividing up aspects of ourselves or the world, there are limits to this arrangement of mind (reason), heart (emotion), soul (spirit), and strength (will). Are our emotional and rational responses to the world truly separate? Do we understand ourselves well enough to know when our reactions to the world are primarily emotional or primarily rational? Do we really know what we mean when we talk about the spiritual dimension of life? Is the free will required for all of this struggle a reality or an illusion? Philosophers and theologians have pondered and argued these questions for centuries without clear resolution. Completely new insights are unlikely to emerge here; maybe there are no truly original insights to be had by anyone. Instead, we can use the categories of mind, heart, soul, and strength as a framework to puzzle through the questions and struggle with our obligations.

For me, the story is anchored in my decision to join the congregation at St. Andrew's Presbyterian Church, the congregation's decision to accept me, an attempt by others in the denomination to expel me for articulating a nontraditional theology, and the aftermath of that struggle. I begin with that story.

MY
STORY

PRESBYTERIAN
FOLLIES

Throughout my childhood I attended a Presbyterian church, trudging off to Sunday school as a youngster, then to church services when I got older. I don't want to be overly dramatic, but this early experience with church was life-threatening—I was bored, nearly to death. All this culminated at age fourteen in the confirmation process and a religious-education class, an endeavor to which I paid little attention. In my life I have cheated on only one test: the exam required to pass that confirmation class, out of desperation so that I would not have to endure the process a second time. For that sin, I have neither sought nor been granted absolution.

My participation in this social ritual was decidedly not voluntary; I was told I would do all this by my parents, which was not unusual in the world in which I grew up. Most of the kids I knew also went to church because they were instructed to do so by adults, and most of us quit going when our parents decided we were old enough to choose for ourselves. Growing up in a middle-of-the-road Protestant church in the Midwest, I experienced church as a boring social club and religion as a banal approach to life. Literature and music, politics and philosophy all seemed far more fruitful and exciting paths to explore.

So in my adult life, the thought of interaction with organized religion has always come with many negative associations. My first visit to St. Andrew's Presbyterian Church came shortly after I arrived in Austin, Texas, in 1992. A friend who had noticed the church's progressive politics, especially on lesbian and gay rights, had started attending, and he suggested I drop by. I went to one Sunday service but wasn't much interested in church at that point in my life and didn't return. I took note of the progressive nature of the place and its pastor, and over the years I paid attention whenever the Reverend Jim Rigby popped up in the news, usually as a result of his support for gay rights or reproductive rights. Those efforts often landed Rigby in hot water with church officials and led to one (failed) attempt to strip him of his ordination.

So when Rigby sent me an email to express support for an antiwar op-ed piece I had written after September 11, 2001, I responded with a note about my respect for his work. That led to a lunch to discuss our mutual interests, which developed into a working relationship around progressive political projects and an ongoing conversation about politics and religion. Rigby and the St. Andrew's congregation offered a space and support for a variety of political programs there—speakers, film screenings, and organizing meetings. Over the course of several years, I became a regular visitor, though I still thought of myself as completely secular and never considered becoming a member of any church. I enjoyed working with the St. Andrew's congregation, and they seemed comfortable having me around as their resident radical secular affiliate, but no one ever suggested I should sign up; it's an inviting congregation, but not a proselytizing one.

MOVING TOWARDS MEMBERSHIP

My relationship to St. Andrew's might have continued on that track if Rigby hadn't asked whether I might be interested in preaching a sermon during a Sunday service. I told him that I didn't think of myself as a preacher but that I would be happy to do it. Rigby got the approval of the Session (the church elders, elected by the members as the governing body of the congregation), and in November 2005 I delivered a sermon to the St. Andrew's congregation titled "Hope Is for the Weak: The Challenge of a Broken World." I wrote it as a talk, not unlike the many other political talks I have given in recent years, but it turned out that whatever my intentions, I delivered it as a sermon. At some point during the service I realized that the context of delivery mattered, and that I was speaking as a lay preacher—I was, in fact, preaching. I went into the St. Andrew's pulpit that morning thinking I knew what I was doing, but in the doing of it I moved into a space I had not expected and that was not entirely familiar to me. The message of the sermon—that we had to acknowledge our weakness if we were to hold onto hope, so that we could be "human in the deepest sense, turning neither from the pain of this broken world nor from the joy that Creation offers us"—seemed to be well received by the congregation. But as I finished, I was less focused on the people there than on myself. I was feeling things I typically didn't feel while giving my political talks.

When I sat down in the pew after I finished, I tried to make some sense of this internal process. As the service proceeded, I leaned forward to Rigby in the pew in front of me and said, "This will sound odd, but I would like to go back to the pulpit at the

end of the service and lead the congregation in the Lord's Prayer."
This was not on the schedule, and in fact the Lord's Prayer was
not part of a typical St. Andrew's service. I hadn't prayed the
Lord's Prayer since childhood, and in that moment I was not sure
exactly why I wanted to do it. I wasn't even sure I remembered the
whole prayer. Rigby reminded me that at St. Andrew's they did
not use sexist language (so the reference to "Our Father" would
have to be adjusted) but didn't hesitate to allow me back in front
of the congregation. I stepped up to the podium and explained to
the people there that I felt a strong desire to speak this prayer with
them, and I began.

"Our Creator, who art in heaven, hallowed be thy name."

As I spoke those words, at least one person gasped, I assume
out of surprise that a secular political activist would venture into
such a traditional prayer. I can't blame people for that reaction;
I was surprised at myself.

"Thy kingdom come, thy will be done, on earth as it is in
heaven."

I stumbled a bit, as I found the rhythm for the words that
were familiar but had gone unspoken for so long.

"Give us this day our daily bread and forgive us our trespasses as
we forgive those who trespass against us."

As I spoke the words, I struggled to hold back tears that were
coming from someplace I didn't understand.

"And lead us not into temptation, but deliver us from evil,

for thine is the kingdom and the power and the glory forever. Amen."

I sat down, shaking ever so slightly, and wondering. My recitation of the Lord's Prayer did not spark an epiphany. I did not feel magically transformed, nor did I have some new sense of the presence of God, Jesus, or the Holy Spirit. It was an intense, but not a mystical, experience. Still, I had felt something that had to do with the power of an often-repeated prayer, spoken collectively. I felt the sense of peace that can come when we let go of control (or the illusion of control) and accept our place in a group, with its collective energy. I felt as if I was part of that congregation in a new way, and I couldn't deny that it felt good.

I left St. Andrew's that day not with a new set of beliefs but with a new experience, one that deserved attention and consideration. After a few days, I asked Rigby whether St. Andrew's might consider me as a candidate for regular membership. I made it clear that I still did not believe in the orthodox conception of God or in the divinity of Christ, but that I felt something that led me to want to move into membership. Rigby explained that new members were not expected to repeat by rote a specific profession of faith but instead were encouraged to craft a statement that reflected their own ideas. That seemed sensible to me, and I wrote a statement in which I endorsed the core principles in Christ's teaching, stated my intention to work to deepen my understanding and practice of the universal love at the heart of those principles, and pledged to be a responsible member of the church and of the larger community. In December 2005 I stood before that congregation, offered that profession, and was accepted as a member. A fair number of people gasped this time.

Shortly after joining St. Andrew's, I wrote about the process, on the hunch that I was not the only person with a progressive secular worldview who was struggling to understand what role religion might play in striving for a better world. In March 2006 I published an essay that ran in two newspapers (one in Houston, Texas, and another in Mumbai, India) and on a number of web sites under the title "Why I Am a Christian (Sort Of)." That piece began:

> I don't believe in God. I don't believe Jesus Christ was the son of a God that I don't believe in, nor do I believe Jesus rose from the dead to ascend to a heaven that I don't believe exists. Given these positions, this year I did the only thing that seemed sensible: I formally joined a Christian church. [17]

I went on to describe myself as "a Christian, sort of. A secular Christian. A Christian atheist, perhaps. But, in a deep sense, I would argue, a real Christian." I was upfront about my political motivations in joining a church: In addition to the personal reasons for becoming a member of St. Andrew's, I was searching for the language that would be most effective in a country where upwards of 75 percent of the population identifies as Christian.[18] I went on to suggest that my decision might not seem so strange given that certain core principles,

---

17 Robert Jensen, "Why I Am a Christian (Sort Of)," AlterNet, March 10, 2006. http://www.alternet.org/story/33236/

18 For statistics, see the "U.S. Religious Landscape Survey" produced by the Pew Forum on Religion and Public Life. http://religions.pewforum.org/reports

such as some version of the Golden Rule, are shared among most theological and secular philosophies. Joining a church and emphasizing those commonalities, it seemed to me, was one way of trying to overcome sectarian divisions and pursue a social-justice agenda.

I ended that essay with these thoughts:

> In his 1927 lecture "Why I Am Not a Christian," the philosopher Bertrand Russell said: "A good world . . . needs a fearless outlook and a free intelligence. It needs hope for the future, not looking back all the time toward a past that is dead."
>
> I couldn't agree more, and I joined a Christian church to be part of that hope for the future, to struggle to make religion a force that can help usher into existence a world in which we can imagine living in peace with each other and in sustainable relation to the nonhuman world.
>
> Such a task requires a fearlessness and intelligence beyond what we have mustered to date, but it also requires a faith in our ability to achieve it.
>
> That is why I am a Christian.

Perhaps I was naïve, but I published the essay with no expectation that it would be controversial. I knew many people who did not hold traditional theological beliefs yet considered themselves religious, and I didn't think that my particular recounting of those struggles would attract much attention beyond progressive circles, where the main criticism often comes from secular comrades who can't understand why I bother with church. But I underestimated the fervor with which traditional forces within my denomination would feel a need to police the boundaries of faith, and before too long the conservative Presbyterian websites and bloggers had picked up on my piece and were making noise about how St. Andrew's had gone too far in admitting an atheist.[19] Compounding the controversy was the fact that this incident came shortly after Rigby had successfully defended himself against denunciations from many of the same conservatives for performing commitment ceremonies for lesbian and gay couples; it's hard not to assume that lots of these folks had an interest in coming after St. Andrew's again. As one conservative commentator put it, "The loss of a biblical vision for the local church is one of the greatest tragedies of our times, leading to a weakened Christian witness and a deadly theological confusion both within and without the church."[20]

And so the theological battle was on, moving the story from St. Andrew's to the presbytery, which is the first level of bureaucracy in the Presbyterian Church (USA). In our case, that's Mission Presbytery, responsible for setting policy for 157 churches in south and central Texas. According to the chairman of the presbytery's Committee on Ministry, the problem was that a church had "received into membership an individual who, according to his own writings, claims neither to believe in God nor to believe that Jesus Christ is who our historic Christian tradition and Scripture claim him to be."[21] That led to the Committee on Ministry dispatching a "listening team" to meet with members of the St. Andrew's Session, and the report of that team—which

19 For example, The Layman Online, http://www.layman.org/ and the now-closed A Classical Presbyterian, http://classicalpresbyterian.blogspot.com/.

20 Albert Mohler, "Why He is Not a Christian—An Atheist Joins a Church," AlbertMohler.com, May 1, 2006. http://www.albertmohler.com/commentary_read.php?cdate=2006-05-01

21 John H. Adams, "Committee investigates membership status of 'Christian-atheist,'" The Layman Online, March 27, 2006. http://www.layman.org/MajorIssues.aspx?article=18357

seemed to do more talking than listening—resulted in censure motions that the full presbytery took up at the next scheduled meeting a few months later.

DELIBERATING ON MY SOUL

So in June 2006 I found myself sitting in a church in San Antonio, listening to several hundred delegates (the ordained ministers in the presbytery and lay representatives from each church) discuss the state of my soul. After representatives of the Committee on Ministry presented the "evidence" of St. Andrew's errors, Rigby was given fifteen minutes to respond, and then delegates to the meeting were allowed to speak from the floor. Weeks before the meeting, presbytery officials had made it clear to Rigby that I would not be allowed to speak, either from the podium or from the floor, though no clear reason was offered. My membership was the subject of the debate, but presbytery officials decided I must remain mute during others' assessment of my faith, which ranged from angry denunciations (not just of me, but also of Rigby and St. Andrew's) to loving support (not just of me, but also of all who doubt and seek). Some people concluded I was no way, no how, any kind of Christian, while others described me as struggling to find faith. One woman, near tears, said she believed that I had already been born again.

It was one of the most surreal afternoons of my life. As I sat with a dozen St. Andrew's members and listened, it became increasingly clear the whole charade had nothing to do with me but was an assertion of dominance by those who wanted—or needed—clear answers to inherently perplexing questions about the meaning of the label "Christian." I assume the reason I was not allowed to speak was that the folks in charge of policing the boundaries of acceptable answers to those questions did not want delegates to see me as real person; better to keep me out of sight so that I could remain an abstraction in most people's minds.

Whatever the motivations of the defenders of orthodoxy, they carried the day. By a vote of 155 to 114, the presbytery instructed St. Andrew's to

A. Declare that the reception of Robert Jensen into active membership was "irregular" and thus void.
B. Direct St. Andrew's session to move Robert Jensen to the "Baptized" Role [a status typically reserved for children awaiting confirmation].
C. Direct the session of St. Andrew's to work with representatives of COM [the Committee on Ministry] to create a constitutionally appropriate process for receiving members.
D. Encourage the session of St. Andrew's, if it so chooses, to re-examine Robert Jensen, if he so desires, according to the process developed by the session and representatives of COM.

From the beginning of the controversy, I had made it clear to Rigby and the St. Andrew's congregation that I would back off if they decided they didn't want to fight the presbytery on this. In some sense, whether or not I was a formal member didn't much matter to me; I would have continued participating in the life of St. Andrew's and would have considered myself part of the community. But the clear consensus of the Session was that the principle mattered and they would not ask me to step back.

But I can't say that the discussion that day and the vote didn't affect me. When the presbytery vote was announced, many of the St. Andrew's members I was sitting with were angry and frustrated. In that specific moment I was calm, reassuring people who reached out to support me that I was fine and they need not worry. But as we filed out of the church, I slipped away from the group to look for a place to be alone for a moment, to sort through my reactions and start crafting my response. Behind the building I leaned up against a stone wall and slid down to the ground to sit and catch my breath. And there, after just a few seconds of being alone, I began to cry. At first I assumed it was an understandable release of emotional energy after a long and intense day, but the tears didn't stop. It wasn't just that I had been rejected, though rejection of any kind can hurt, even when it's political or philosophical and not personal. I don't think my tears were about me. I was crying for something that I think had to do with a fallen world—that I didn't quite grasp in that moment and still don't fully understand.

THE INEVITABLE COMPROMISE

After the dust settled from the presbytery meeting, St. Andrew's filed an appeal with the synod, the next level up in the bureaucracy. That appeal was denied on technical grounds, but in the meantime a variety of people in the presbytery realized that it might be in everyone's best interest to find a way to resolve the dispute without forcing a full-scale doctrinal showdown. Because I had been confirmed in a Presbyterian church as a youth, the presbytery could recognize the transfer of my membership from one congregation to another, conveniently removing the issue of my status. That left on the table only the question of St. Andrew's policy on accepting members, which led to a symposium at the local seminary to discuss appropriate standards for membership in September 2007. After that gathering, Mission Presbytery voted to send to the denomination's 2008 General Assembly a proposal to establish the following question-and-answer ritual for membership candidates:

Question: Trusting in the gracious mercy of God, do you turn from the ways of sin and renounce evil and its power in the world?
Answer: I do.

Who is your Lord and Savior?
Jesus Christ is my Lord and Savior.

Will you be Christ's faithful disciple, obeying his Word and showing his love?
I will, with God's help.

Will you be an faithful member of this congregation, share in its worship and ministry through your prayers and gifts, your study and service, and so fulfill your calling to be a disciple of Jesus Christ?
I will, with God's help.

By the time that proposal made its way through the Presbyterian Church (USA)'s Church Polity Committee, the language had been softened. The final version, which the General Assembly approved by a voice vote, retains the terms "Lord and Savior" but is vague on specifics:

After new members are examined, affirming their faith in Jesus Christ as Lord and Savior, and are received by the Session, whether by profession of faith, certificate of transfer, or reaffirmation of faith, they shall be presented to and welcomed by the congregation during a service of worship where they shall make a public profession of their faith in Jesus Christ as Lord and Savior, as do confirmands [candidates for confirmation].[22]

None of this should have been surprising, for my membership and profession of faith highlighted two basic aspects of Protestantism that are inherently in conflict. Unlike the Catholic Church, no hierarchy exists in Protestant churches to threaten excommunication and impose orthodoxy of belief (though even with that centralized power, Catholic leaders have notoriously little power to make people accept doctrine on controversial subjects such as contraception and abortion). The notion of a "priesthood of all believers" has meant that Protestants define their faith in an individual relationship with God, in the context of local community; congregational autonomy is highly valued. But it's also obvious that any group (religious or otherwise) that is to remain a recognizable group has to have some standards for membership, or else membership becomes meaningless. This tension forces a question that many would prefer not to face: What does it mean to claim to be a Presbyterian, or a Protestant, or a Christian? Does it require one to believe the term "God" describes an identifiable force, entity, or being in the world? Does it require one to believe the resurrection of Jesus was a historical fact? Or can one be a Presbyterian, a Protestant, or a Christian and believe, for example, that "God" is simply a term for the energy that gives rise to life and that the resurrection should be understood symbolically?

---

22 Presbyterian Church (USA), "On Amending G-5.0200 to Add the Vows of Membership to the Book of Order." http://www.pc-biz.org/Explorer. aspx?m=ro&id=1425

What if we were to walk through the Protestant churches of the United States today, especially the centrist-to-liberal churches, and ask such questions of every member? How many would be left in the pews if all had to profess a belief in the supernatural claims about God and Jesus? I won't venture an estimate, but my hunch is that the collection plates would be considerably lighter if churches were to expel all the skeptics and all who held nonorthodox views. I can only speculate, but my guess is that these observations are commonplace, which is why the boundary police from the Committee on Ministry initially felt it was important to punish a congregation that acknowledged the more complex reality of the contemporary church. Only when it appeared their plan would backfire did they step back, recognizing the danger of raising such questions. But even with that danger, orthodox forces couldn't let it rest.

THE FUTURE

As I write this, I remain a member in good standing of St. Andrew's, with no further disruption of that status expected. I continue to help organize programs there, with a focus on both the big-picture philosophical and theological questions, as well as contemporary political issues. I have filled in as the leader of adult Sunday class and preached a couple more times. My friendships and associations with people from the church continue to deepen. I attend Sunday services, and when it comes time for the hymns I shuffle nervously because I have such a horrendous singing voice. In short, I'm a pretty average middle-aged white American male churchgoer.

My basic beliefs about the concept of God haven't changed much since I joined St. Andrew's, though I no longer use the terms "atheist" or "agnostic" to describe myself. That's in part because since this phase of my life began there has been a renewed public discussion about atheism, sparked in large part by the publication of several books, all of which leave me unsatisfied.[23] These authors, routinely referred to as the "new atheists" in media reports, offer much useful critical analysis of the supernatural claims of religion and the often destructive effects of religion, but they strike me—in their public comments as well as in their writing—as smug and self-satisfied (with some variation in the group; it would be difficult for anyone to match Hitchens's level of smugness).

For example, one manifestation of this discussion has been the notion of "brights," people who define themselves as having a "naturalistic worldview . . . free of supernatural and mystical elements."[24] I first came across the term in Dennett's 2003 *New York Times* op-ed, and though I find his book *Breaking the Spell* helpful in many ways, I can't imagine attaching myself to any group that labels itself as brights—even if it's intended not as a boast but "a proud avowal of an inquisitive world view."[25] Maybe that makes me one of the "dims." Beyond that, it's not clear what category I belong in, given Dennett's definition of religions as "social systems whose participants avow belief in a supernatural agent or agents whose approval is to be sought" and the core phenomenon of religion as an invocation of "gods who

---

23 Richard Dawkins, *The God Delusion* (New York: Houghton Mifflin, 2006), Daniel C. Dennett, *Breaking the Spell: Religion as a Natural Phenomenon* (New York: Penguin, 2006), Sam Harris, *The End of Faith* (New York: W. W. Norton, 2004) and *Letter to a Christian Nation* (New York: Vintage/Random House, 2006), and Christopher Hitchens, *God Is Not Great* (New York: Twelve/Hachette, 2007). For a detailed critique of these writers, see Chris Hedges, *I Don't Believe in Atheists* (New York: Free Press, 2008).

24 "What is a bright?" http://www.the-brights.net/

25 Daniel C. Dennett, "The Bright Stuff," *New York Times*, July 12, 2003.

are effective agents in real time, and who play a central role in the way the participants think about what they ought to do."[26] If some of us identify as Christian but have a radically different conception of God, are we really Christian? Are we even religious? It appears that the orthodox folks from the presbytery and the new atheists might agree on, if nothing else, how to define religion—narrowly.

But more important than my dissatisfaction with the new atheists is my positive experience at St. Andrew's. I continue to read, think, and discuss these issues with my pastor, fellow church members, and a wider public. I have had engaging discussions with a number of progressive thinkers from other faiths that have deepened my identification as a member of a Christian church. In short, my core beliefs haven't changed much, but I don't feel like an atheist or agnostic.

At the same time as my understanding of theology has deepened, so has my understanding of the nature of the crises we face in this world and my awareness of their magnitude. Those political and ecological concerns have made me even more interested in theology, out of the belief that we humans face problems that will severely test our capacities in the coming decades. In the remainder of this book I want to explore the connections between the material and spiritual, the philosophical and theological, the political and religious. I don't pretend to have definitive answers, but my own sense of the questions has deepened by examining political issues within a theological framework. So I return to the first of the commandments, the task of loving God with all our mind, heart, soul, and strength.

---

26 Dennett, *Breaking the Spell*, pp. 9–12.

PART I

MIND

THE CHAOS
OF TRUTH

My friend Oscar Brockett, a professor for more than fifty years, is fond of reminding me of the importance of definitions. "Allow me to define the terms, and I will win every argument we have," he says. Brock was talking about arguments in the classical sense of the term from the study of rhetoric, not the silly shouting matches that we see and hear on most talk shows, for example. In an argument, one offers premises to support a conclusion. In evaluating conclusions we must look at the underlying assumptions, the quality of the evidence, and the logical progression to the conclusion. And, as my friend reminds me, we should pay close attention to definitions of terms.

Our evaluation of arguments about religion is not solely rational, of course, but the application of reason should be part of the evaluation. As the cliché goes, if God gave us a brain, we should use it to think, including about God. So in examining the first commandment to love God, we might start by using our minds to think about how we define those two terms, "love" and "God." Immediately we can see a problem.

When we talk about loving a person, place, thing, or idea in our everyday lives, we have direct knowledge of the object of our love, and our love flows from what that knowledge sparks in us. We have some sense of who the person is, where the place is, what the idea is. We are drawn to qualities that we can identify. It matters not what kind of love we have in mind, whether we are referring to *eros* (sexual or romantic love), *philia* (the love in friendship), or *agape* (a more spiritual sense of love). I love my partner, my son, my friends, the prairie where I was born, the essays of James Baldwin, the philosophy of radical democracy. In each case, whatever the kind of love under examination, I know quite a bit about the person, place, thing, or idea for which I am proclaiming my love.

In fact, we truly love only whom and what we know well. When we talk about love in the abstract—our love for all the world, for example—it tends to sound a bit empty, an important point to which I'll return in later chapters. We may believe we have a responsibility to be kind and decent to all in the world, but we understand the difference between that kind of moral connection to others and a more emotional connection that comes with the love we experience directly in our lives. We tend to have deeper feelings for the people around us, the places we know more intimately, the ideas that we have grappled with.

If this deep sense of love requires knowledge of the object of our affection, we're in trouble when we are commanded to love God, if God is understood as an entity, force, or being. We may strive to love God as deeply as possible, but the defining quality of the idea of God is that we cannot know God. In fact, one of the few things that almost everyone who believes in God shares is a recognition that God is so far beyond our knowing, so much more expansive than our capacity to understand, that we lack the language even to try to begin to describe God in any coherent sense. We are told God is infinite and eternal, eternally simple yet infinitely complex, perfect and immutable. That is all well and good, but it doesn't get us much closer to a clear understanding. God is omniscient, omnipotent, and omnipresent. Okay, I get it: God is powerful, but in ways we can't really comprehend. Oh, and by the way, God is incorporeal, taking no form and especially no human form. Of course traditionally God is referred to as masculine, as if "he" were one of us and just happens to be male, even though the incorporeal nature of God must mean he or she or it can't really be a "he" because he or she or it has no form that is like anything we know and therefore should be beyond gendered pronouns.

The more people try to describe and define God, the more it becomes clear the idea of God is beyond description and definition. So to claim to know God would be an act of incredible hubris: God appears to be unknowable. And if we can truly love only that which we know, how are we to love God?

Maybe that's why people keep trying to come up with some definition of God, out of a desire to know what it is we are to love. In this quest, people paradoxically speak of God as another term for "love." In the Bible this is expressed directly in the First Letter of John:

[7] Beloved, let us love one another; for love is of God, and he who loves is born of God and knows God. [8] He who does not love does not know God; for God is love.

[1 JOHN 4:7–8]

and

[16] So we know and believe the love God has for us. God is love, and he who abides in love abides in God, and God abides in him.

[1 JOHN 4:16]

In contemporary culture, the phrase "God is love" is common across the political and theological spectrum. For example, Martin Luther King Jr. quoted that passage from St. John in his speech criticizing the Vietnam War in 1967, in support of the call for "a worldwide fellowship that lifts neighborly concern beyond one's tribe, race, class, and nation."[27] Nearly four decades later, a considerably more conservative theologian, Pope Benedict, used the phrase (in Latin, *Deus caritas est*) as the title and focus of his first encyclical letter released in 2006.[28]

But if God is a synonym for love, then the commandment to "love God" would translate as "love love." At the risk of sounding sacrilegious, that gets us pretty close to the lyrics of a whole lot of pop songs. "Love, love, love," the Beatles sang. "All you need is love." It makes for a catchy tune, but it doesn't do much to clarify what we mean by God.

So we are commanded to love a God we cannot ever really know, and what we seem to know about God is that God is love, leading to the notion that we must love love. If this feels a bit like a hall of mirrors, well, that might be because it is. Cynics might suggest that the hall was designed this way deliberately by religion specialists (preachers and theologians) to make sure they would always have work—if an idea is appealing but incomprehensible, it will take a steady flow of sermons and books, church services and seminars to explain the unexplainable. These specialists do their best to spin workable accounts of

---

27 Martin Luther King Jr., *A Testament of Hope: The Essential Writings and Speeches of Martin Luther King Jr.*, James M. Washington, ed. (New York: HarperCollins, 1991), p. 242.

28 "Deus Caritas Est," Encyclical Letter of the Supreme Pontiff Benedict XVI, released January 25, 2006. http://www.catholic.org/clife/publications/b16_encyclical_godislove.pdf

these things, but those attempts never seem to clarify much for me. That sends me to back to basics.

GOD AND/AS MYSTERY

Returning to the St. Andrew's story: When I was told I would not be allowed to speak during the presbytery's heresy trial, I wrote a statement about my beliefs so that delegates could have some sense of my views. At the heart of that statement were these thoughts on the trinity:

> *On God*: I believe God is a name we give to the mystery of the world that is beyond our capacity to understand. I believe that the energy of the universe is ordered by forces I cannot comprehend.

> *On Jesus*: I believe Christ offered a way into that mystery that still has meaning today.

> *On the Holy Ghost*: There are moments in my life when I feel a connection to other people and to Creation that rides a spirit which flows through me yet is beyond me. I believe that Holy Spirit can only be nurtured in real community, where people make commitments to each other.

This approach to the concept of God not only rejects a naïve and illusory biblical literalism but also challenges the conception of God that many moderate Christians hold. The key is whether we refer to God as *a mystery* or simply as *mystery*, and the difference between those two formulations is crucial. The first, with the indefinite article, implies that God is an entity, force, or being with some shape, but that his or her or its contours are beyond our capacity to fully comprehend and chart. The thing that God is, is a mystery to us, but God is something, some kind of thing that, if we had the capacity, we could describe. The second formulation suggests that God is simply the name we give to that which is beyond our capacity to understand. God is not a mystery but rather another name for mystery—for the vast, unexplainable mystery of the world around as we swirl among those billions of stars, as well as the mystery inside as those billions of cells interact to create us.

If God is not *a* mystery but rather is *another name for* mystery, then there is no trap. The command to love God can be understood as simply another way of saying that we must strive to love the mystery around us and in us, rather than to be afraid of all that we cannot understand. We certainly know that mystery and bump up against it daily. I can strive to deepen my sense of that mystery, and I can have reverence for it. I can have a deep love for the wonder that such mystery produces, whether the mystery centers on me, on the nature of my relationship to other people, or on the nature of my relationship to the world. With this conception of God we are not striving to love what we cannot know, but coming to terms with the fact that we will never know and embracing our place in the world. To seek to always love God means, from this view, to seek always to accept our place in a Creation that will always be mystery, no matter how much science teaches us about specific parts of that Creation around us and in us, through physics and biology. To love God is not a command to stop seeking knowledge, but rather a reminder to have a sense of the limits of our knowledge and to embrace that which is beyond knowledge. Nothing in this view demands that we reject science, but instead reminds us to be aware not only of what science illuminates but also what is beyond its reach.

It's not hard to understand why people in the world before modern science attributed certain things to an idea of God as an entity, or force, or being. Such a concept could be used to explain why the rain fell, the lightning lit up the sky, and the thunder shook the ground beneath them. A God that could intervene in human affairs could be used to explain why people suffered in some instances and prospered in others. That we now have other ways—natural science, philosophy, history, the social sciences—to guide our understanding does not mean we need to scrap those stories our ancestors told. Instead, we can reframe those stories to find other levels of wisdom in them. The poet Muriel Rukeyser reminds us of the importance of this when she writes, "The universe is made of stories, not of atoms."[29]

Even with the advances in science, in a deep sense the universe remains mystery to us, and we understand that mystery through stories. "God" is a term for mystery explored in story. To make such a shift in our understanding of God is not to lose faith, but to understand the dynamic nature of faith. If God is the name for what we cannot know, our love for God is an expression of our knowledge of our limits and of our commitment to living in the world within those limits. Our love for God reminds us of the need for humility. In this sense, God is a way of reminding ourselves that while we are a clever species, this cleverness has not only improved our lives but gotten us into considerable trouble.

So to return to my central thesis: There is no God, and more than ever we all need to worship the One True Gods. My claim is that we should leave behind the conception of God as an entity, force, or being, giving up the desire to find such a God. In the

---

29 Muriel Rukeyser, "The Speed of Darkness," in *The Speed of Darkness* (New York: Random House, 1968), stanza 9, lines 3–4.

concluding chapter, I'll return to the more complex question of the One True Gods.

THE CHAOS OF TRUTH

We humans appear to be the only life form on the planet that fusses about truth. As far as we can know, oak trees and wolves don't spend much time considering whether the understanding of the world that guides their actions is true; it appears that oak trees and wolves go about their business in the world without reflection upon the nature of truth. We humans may at times wish we were a bit more like oak trees and wolves; this quality we call consciousness is, as that cliché goes, a blessing and a curse.

This struggle for truth is at least in part rooted in the fact that when we modern humans with the big brain look out on the world, we see incredible complexity that dwarfs our ability to catalog and analyze. The world we see is chaotic, especially in the modern era when we can see (or, at least, see a representation of) so much of the world through mass media and have a direct experience of (or, at least, brush up against) so much of the world because of relatively rapid transit. But the cleverness we humans have developed to control many aspects of our environment is a bit of a trap; it leads us to believe we can understand the world, but then the world inevitably proves too complex for our understanding. It's as if we are the victims of a cosmic bait-and-switch scam—we know just enough to seem to be able to control the world, and then the world reminds us of our limits. We build nuclear power plants and then wonder what to do with the deadly waste. We dig for coal and drill for oil, then scratch our heads as the planet heats up.

Wes Jackson, a planet geneticist who left conventional academic life to cofound the Land Institute to pursue projects about sustainable agriculture and sustainable culture, suggests that we would be wise to recognize this human condition—our basic ignorance. His point is that whatever our technical and scientific prowess, we are—and always will be—far more ignorant than knowledgeable, and therefore it would be sensible for us to adopt "an ignorance-based worldview" that could help us understand these limits.[30] Acknowledging our basic ignorance does not mean we should revel in the ways humans can act stupidly, but rather we should be spurred to recognize that we have an obligation to act as intelligently as possible, keeping in mind not only what we know but also how much we don't know. Such humility is implicit not only in the dominant faith systems today, but also in traditional and indigenous systems. Humility is also the key lesson that we should take from the Enlightenment and modern science—a contentious claim, perhaps, given the way in which modern science tends to overreach. The crucial Enlightenment insight, however, is not that humans can understand everything in the universe through reason, but that we can give up attempts to know everything and be satisfied with knowing only what we can know. That is, we can be content in making it up as we go along, cautiously, aware that we often will be wrong. That is the real lesson of the scientific revolution, and one of the tragedies of the modern world is that too few have learned that lesson. The conception of God-as-mystery is a healthy corrective

---

30 Wes Jackson, "Toward an Ignorance-Based Worldview," *The Land Report*, Spring 2005, pp. 14–16. http://www.landinstitute.org/vnews/display.v/ART/2004/10/03/42c0db19e37f4

See also Bill Vitek and Wes Jackson, eds., *The Virtues of Ignorance: Complexity, Sustainability, and the Limits of Knowledge* (Lexington: University Press of Kentucky, 2008).

to human arrogance, providing theological support for the igno-rance-based worldview that Jackson prescribes.

We should remember that this lesson also is at the heart of the Christian creation story. Following Jackson's analysis, we might consider reading Adam and Eve's banishment in chapters two and three of Genesis as a warning that hubris is our tragic flaw. In the garden, God told them they could eat freely of every tree but the tree of knowledge of good and evil. This need not be understood as a command that people must stay stupid, but only that we resist the temptation to believe we are godlike and can manipulate the complexity of the world. Human arrogance of that type is epitomized by a boast made in 2000 by Richard Dawkins, one of the "new atheists." As a scientist, he certainly understands the contingent nature of scientific inquiry, yet he made the claim that "our brains . . . are big enough to see into the future and plot long-term consequences."[31] Such a statement is a reminder that human egos are typically larger than brains, which emphasizes this dramatic need for humility.

Nothing in this view argues for giving up on the idea of truth or humans' capacity to know the many things that we can trust that we know. It is not a plea to abandon science and seek answers purely on nonrational grounds, but rather a reminder that we should under-stand our limits. Nor does this view demand that we give up our struggle to know the mystery that is beyond our rational capacity. It is not a plea to abandon spirituality and confine ourselves only to what can be safely known through science, but rather a reminder not to create answers simply because we want answers.

As we sort through this, we also must never forget our moral obligation: We are limited, but our limits don't relieve us of our duty

---

31 Richard Dawkins, "An Open Letter to Prince Charles," May 21, 2000. http://www.edge.org/3rd_culture/prince/prince_index.html

to act in the world in ways we can defend as ethical, as consistent with human flourishing in harmony with the non-human world. Our intellectual and spiritual limits don't mean that the suffering of others is irrelevant because we can't be sure how to alleviate it. Nor does it mean that we can turn our backs on the obligation to live in harmony with the rest of the planet, even if it appears that we have intervened in the ecological health of the planet in a fashion that may have gone beyond the point of no return.

This conception of God and knowledge asks us to grow up and buck up, to deal with our frailty both with humility for what we don't (and can't) know and responsibility for what we can (and must) do if we are to be fully human. In his first letter to the Corinthians, Paul advised that we face these tasks, anchored as always in love:

[8] Love never ends; as for prophecies, they will pass away; as for tongues, they will cease; as for knowledge, it will pass away. [9] For our knowledge is imperfect and our prophecy is imperfect; [10] but when the perfect comes, the imperfect will pass away.

[1 COR. 13: 8–10]

Whatever we might think is "the perfect," it is not with us here. We live in the imperfect; we struggle with the chaotic. We usually think of our rational faculties as providing us with the ability to deal with the chaos of truth, to provide the order we need to live in a complex world. Conversely, our emotions are seen as a source of even greater chaos, an aspect of ourselves that is generally out of control. I want to argue just the opposite: The chaos of truth is a product of the rational, and whatever clarity of truth we can achieve is produced not in our minds but in our hearts.

PART II

HEART

THE CLARITY
OF TRUTH

Early in my graduate study at the University of Minnesota, I was in the office of my favorite professor, Naomi Scheman, who taught courses in epistemology and feminist philosophy. The intersection of those two areas—how we come to know things and make knowledge claims, and the way patriarchy structures how we think about self and society—were of particular relevance for my research on the feminist critique of pornography. In a conversation about how to assess the effects of pornography on individuals and society, Naomi and I were talking about the role of emotions in understanding such things. The problem with emotions, I suggested, was that they were too personal and couldn't be communicated with enough specificity to be the basis for discussions about the social world and public policy. Emotions mattered, I argued, but they couldn't have a serious role in a public conversation about the subject.

Scheman look at me, rather bemused, and asked the best question a teacher can ask when a student says something stupid: "Why do you say that?"

I don't recall my response in the moment, but over the course of that year I spent a lot of time pondering her question, and eventually acknowledged something that is obvious to most women I have met: I had wanted to believe that emotions were only personal and inherently unreliable, and therefore should be kept out of public debate, because I was afraid of my own emotions and the emotions of others. If emotions could not be trusted as evidence about how the world works, then emotions need not be part of our discussions of that world, hence there would be no need to think about my own emotional life or take seriously the emotional reactions of others. This leads to important questions about many aspects of men's behavior in the world, but for our purposes here I want to focus on the need I had at that point in my life to believe that our rational faculties could provide us with all that we require to understand the world. I saw emotion as fundamentally irrational and reason as the only hope humans had to come to deeper knowledge. I believed that emotions created chaos, and through reason we could achieve clarity.

At first glance, that seems like a sensible proposition, given the destructive capacity of our emotions. We can easily catalog numerous harms to self and others that have come when our emotions have run amok; in the grip of strong emotions, people can say and do amazingly cruel things. Our emotions do seem to lead us to some pretty crazy behavior at times.

But, even with those dangers, I now think I got it wrong about the role of emotion, in two ways. First, I mistakenly thought of reason and emotion as wholly separate functions. Second, if we do think of these two categories as distinct, it is in fact reason that more often creates chaos, while our best hope for clarity is our emotions. When we want to deepen our understanding of how we behave in the chaotic world in which we live, the best place to begin is usually with the emotional. Without that understanding of the feelings that drive us, we are likely to go off the rails in trying to understand self and others. It's relatively easy to make up stories in which we explain our actions as the product of rational evaluations of situations, leading us to rational conclusions. Such stories can be comforting, reassuring us that we are in control of ourselves and our world, but to believe them is dangerous.

So if we are to value the way our emotions can guide us, we ask: What does it mean to love God with all our hearts? If we consider the way we can understand the world through our emotions, it's clear that our hearts can pull us in many different directions, some of which can be destructive. Perhaps the most dangerous of the emotions, in terms of religious faith, is fear.

Does the fear of death lead people to profess a rigid faith in God without sufficient reflection? When people recognize that we live in a complex world we can't control, do they seek a theology that offers definitive answers, fearing that we really are powerless in the face of that complexity? Are people afraid that there may be no inherent purpose to human life, forcing us to face the daunting task of constructing meaning ourselves? I certainly have met people who seem to be motivated by these kinds of fears, and in my experience that kind of motivation leads people to gravitate toward dogmatic certainty in religious doctrine. So in discussion of emotion's role in our understanding of the mystery we call God, we should start with fear.

FUNDAMENTALIST FEARS

Several years ago I had an ongoing conversation with a young man who was an evangelical Christian. It was clear that his regular chats with me were proselytizing; at that time I described myself as an atheist, and he clearly hoped that I might accept

Jesus as my savior in the same fashion he did. Whatever his motivation, I found the conversations interesting and educational, a way to understand a bit more about a theology that was, and remains, foreign to me.

One day, which turned out to be the last time we talked, the discussion turned to the biblical interpretation. He attended a church in which people believed that the Bible had plain meaning and that anyone who applied common sense could know that meaning with relatively little disagreement. From their perspective, the Bible is the word of God and therefore completely inerrant in all aspects or, at least, infallible on matters of faith (I was never clear on which position he held), and God gave us the ability to read and understand without the inherent ambiguity and potential confusion that comes with all other human communication.

So, I asked him, would you and the folks at your church say that there is no interpretation of the text necessary? Yes, he said, we take the Bible literally and don't interpret.

An easy way to press people on this claim is to go to the various passages in the Old Testament that no one takes seriously anymore. For example, when's the last time anyone in the contemporary United States endorsed stoning to death "a stubborn and rebellious son," as is prescribed in Deuteronomy, to make sure that you "purge the evil from your midst"? [Deut. 21:18–21] The meaning seems plain, but people who claim to be "literalists" ignore that particular plain meaning. This reminds us of a simple fact: Everyone who reads any passage, no matter what brand of theology one prefers, is interpreting the text; people never are simply extracting obvious meaning but are always making meaning, deciding what is more or less important and how to understand it. That doesn't suggest that all possible interpretations are equally sensible or valid; that some interpretations won't be more compelling than others, based on moral insights or evidence; that we can't, or shouldn't, make judgments about competing interpretations. It just means that I don't get to trump another's interpretation by claiming mine is self-evident.

But I didn't want to get stuck in a discussion of all the biblical commands that people today don't follow, which tends to lead to claims that the plain meaning of a second passage later in the text trumps the first passage's plain meaning, and so on. How that argument denies the role of interpretation, I'm not sure. But instead of that route, I asked him a simple question about the different kinds of writing in the Bible. There are historical accounts, articulations of divine law, moral teachings, parables, poetry—the Bible speaks in different voices, in many types of literature, yes? He agreed.

I asked him: Do you read the poetry the same way you read the accounts of history? Do you try to understand the parables the same way as a statement about law? Of course not, he said, because each had to be assessed according to the type of writing and the purpose of the passage. So is it fair to say, I continued, that you have what might be called an "interpretive strategy" for how to read different parts of the Bible differently depending on the type of writing? He agreed.

"So what you are contending," I said, "is that you read the Bible with an interpretive strategy, shifting your approach depending on what part of the Bible you are reading, but that you don't interpret the Bible?" After pondering that for a few seconds, he ignored the challenge, repeated earlier statements about the "plain meaning of the Bible," and quickly excused himself. He never came round again to talk, so I never had a chance to ask him about his reaction to my simple query. I suspect the reason he avoided me was equally simple: He was afraid, at two levels.

The first fear leads people to believe that such a varied collection of writings—put together over hundreds of years, translated in and out of various languages, and the subject of internal political struggles over what was and was not to be included in the canon—could have an obvious plain meaning upon which all right-thinking people could agree. That is rooted, I believe, in a fear of a world that is complex beyond our understanding, a fear of the fact that uncertainty is the defining characteristic of human claims to knowledge. In such a world, it's not difficult to see why people would want to believe that there is a source of ultimate understanding that can reveal itself to people, rather than a contingent source of understanding that we must work hard to grasp, knowing that a definitive understanding is always just beyond our grasp. The second fear concerns the reaction to any challenge to such a belief; if the instinct to believe in this fashion is rooted in fear, a challenge to that belief is likely to intensify the fear. It usually is frightening for us all whenever we have to ponder the possibility that a central tenet of our belief system is illogical.

Fundamentalists don't have a monopoly on fear, of course. It stalks us all, in ways personal and theological.

MODERATE FEARS

Within the first month after publishing my essay about joining St. Andrew's, I received several hundred calls and emails, most of them supportive of my position. There also were some from traditional Christians who told me that until I truly accepted Jesus as my lord and savior I had no right to claim to be Christian, while a few secular leftists asked why I was bothering with religion at all. The most amusing letters, unintentionally, were from

Unitarians telling me that I really was a Unitarian but apparently had yet to recognize that. But the most interesting feedback I received was from Christians struggling with their own faith.

One woman who called immediately apologized for bothering me, but clearly wanted to talk. She belonged to a mainstream Presbyterian church in Minnesota, where I had lived several times when I was younger. After we traded a few Minnesota stories to break the ice, she explained that most of the members of her church were pretty conventional theologically and tended to lean centrist-to-liberal in political terms. As we talked, it seemed to me she was heading toward a question but finding it difficult to get there. Finally I said, "Is there anything specific you wanted to know about me or what I believe?" Yes, she said, sounding relieved to finally get to it: "Do you think Jesus really rose from the dead?"

As I got her to say more, it was clear that she was terrified of the question of whether the resurrection was historical fact or could be understood as symbolic. I told her that, of course, no one could prove definitively that Jesus didn't roll back the rock and emerge alive, just as we can't disprove definitively any religion's supernatural claims. But I understood that story—and, in fact, all such claims of Christianity as well as other religions—symbolically, metaphorically, as stories about larger truths. The resurrection story has always struck me, even as a child, as a way of coming to terms with our own eventual death, allowing us to see ourselves as part of something beyond our self. The resurrection story for me is primarily about the suffering we face when we confront power and call out injustice. The fact that other traditions have resurrection stories suggests this is not a distinctive aspect of Christianity but a common part of people's struggle to understand death and the collective spirit. At its core, perhaps the resurrection simply affirms that our connection with others has a component beyond the flesh, that after our bodies are gone we live in memory and spirit, part of a life force that we can't fully comprehend through science or philosophy.

But more interesting to me than my analysis was her understanding, especially about why she was so afraid of the question. As she talked more, it was clear she was struggling with two fears. The first was internally generated. For her entire life, she had been told—and had thought she believed—that if the resurrection was not a historical fact, then Christianity was a lie, a kind of con game. Growing up, and into adulthood, she had been told over and over that the resurrection of Christ was "the ground of our faith," beyond challenge. From memory she repeated to me the last part of the standard version of the Apostle's Creed: "I believe in the Holy Spirit, the holy catholic church, the communion of saints, the forgiveness of sins, the resurrection of the body, and the life everlasting." Without "the resurrection of the body," she asked, could there be "life everlasting"?

As an adult who was reflecting on the diversity of religious traditions, she was questioning why one had to accept the literal fact of the resurrection or be condemned to hell for all eternity. But because she had spent so much of her life assuming that was the case, she was afraid to give up that belief. All I could tell her was that I knew many people who were struggling along with her, that they were kind and decent people committed to their congregations and to the world, and that I couldn't imagine how a loving community could reject that kind of honest searching.

That got us to her second fear, about how her doubts would be received by others. She told me she was scared to talk with folks in the congregation about these questions and conclusions she was reaching. This was not a fundamentalist church, she reminded me, but just from the way people talked she knew that questioning the resurrection wouldn't be well received. I asked if she had any friends in the congregation who might have a position similar to hers. She said that she was fairly certain there were at least some others, but they weren't talking about it either. She had no trouble explaining this fear: I have spent my whole life in this church, and I don't want to get pushed out, she said.

I don't know how representative of contemporary Christians this woman was, or how common her struggle might be today. But my gut feeling is that what she described is likely the state of affairs in most centrist and liberal congregations. In other words, we have congregations full of people with doubt who are afraid of their own thoughts and afraid of the possibility of a hostile reaction from others. That doesn't sound like a healthy state of affairs for any kind of community, religious or secular.

I don't offer these stories about fundamentalist or moderate fears with any haughtiness. I have fears of my own, and I can see how many times in the past those fears led me to believe things that didn't hold up over time. For example, in my early twenties I spent a couple of years immersed in the work of the novelist and essayist Ayn Rand and found her ultralibertarian philosophy appealing. I never joined the cult of believers that often forms around her books, but my own need at the time to believe that I could define myself independent of culture and family—a kind of adolescent desire to claim absolute, and hence illusory, control over self—led me to take seriously a philosophy that, in retrospect, seems not just wrong but childish. It's not just that I now disagree with Rand's moral and political assertions, but that her conception of what it means to be human strikes me as pathological, a strange distortion of our actual psychology. But my fears at the time made those ideas compelling to me.

I have no doubt that today, in ways I cannot see clearly at the moment, my fears affect my ability to understand myself and others as fully as possible. Our view at any moment in time is always partial, and there's no reason to be cocky, even when one is fairly clear about the deficiencies of a competing point of view. In other words, I am confident in my assessment that the position on textual interpretation held by my fundamentalist conversation partner was untenable. I am confident in advising the caller to be bold in raising her questions about the resurrection with others. But that doesn't mean I want to pretend others cannot look at my life and help me identify, and come to terms with, my fears.

With all those caveats, I have no problem not only criticizing, but also denouncing, any theology that keeps us trapped in our fears rather than helping us face them. A theology that requires us to turn away from our own doubts is going to be of little value in helping us cope with the pain of life more generally. How can we love God with all our heart if we are trapped in fear?

What might a less fearful love look and feel like? I want to return to my first claim, that we can find some clarity in the chaos by letting our emotions guide us, as long as fear doesn't derail us. I returned to church in part for emotional reasons, and I continue to find that my most profound experiences in church are emotional, albeit relatively quiet. Discussions of the emotion in Christianity often focus on Pentecostal or charismatic churches and their open displays of ecstatic emotion (especially practices such as speaking in tongues), which is one part of the story. I want to focus on another side of our emotional lives, looking at the ways in which our brokenness can bring us to church, and how church can provide a space to heal.

BROKEN PEOPLE

Much of my public discussion about the decision to join St. Andrew's has focused on the world out there—the call for social justice, the role of church in progressive politics, our responsibility to resist illegitimate authority. Those concerns are at the center of my theology and practice, and I easily could stop there. It's a nice, neat explanation for why I returned to church, one that makes me look smart but not boastful, thoughtful and self-confident, nobly focused on my obligations to others. But it would be an incomplete explanation, for there was another motivation behind my decision to join, one much more personal. It's tempting to ignore this aspect, in part out of a desire to avoid revealing inappropriate personal information that can make others uncomfortable. But it's important to my story to note that in recent years I have begun confronting some unresolved issues from my childhood involving abuse. The details are not important to recount; it's enough to note that it has not been a fun process, and I struggle daily with sadness and anger, confusion and self-doubt. Those who have experience with such things know what that means, and others likely can imagine the contours of the experience.

To leave out this part of my story would be dishonest, and it would gloss over another important motivation that leads people to church: the need for acceptance and love in community when we are scared and lonely, weak and alone. And, of course, at some point we all are scared, lonely, weak, and alone. When struggling with any difficult problem in our lives, we tend to rely on those closest to us. If we are lucky, as I am, we have a supportive and loving partner, good friends, and the resources to hire a competent therapist when a problem goes beyond our friends' ability to help. But what we need in addition to all that is a community in which we can just be. It need not be a church, but a church is one place where people seek that community. In my experience, we humans tend to want to have a place where we know we can go without worrying about how we look that day, a place we can find validation and connection without having to prove that we deserve it at that moment. Church is not the only place where that can happen, and there's no guarantee it will happen in church; despite Christ's admonition against self-serving judgment of others, such judgment happens all too often in churches of all varieties. But whatever our failures, church is one place we seek out such acceptance.

I didn't have a conscious understanding of that when I joined St. Andrew's, but I think I had an intuitive sense that I needed such a place and that St. Andrew's could be such a place for me. In our patriarchal culture, this need can be particularly difficult for us men to acknowledge, out of a fear it will be read as a sign of weakness. But is there anyone who doesn't feel that need at times? And, if we turn away from this need that we feel, what are the consequences? What part of ourselves do we bury to ignore that need?

We need not ignore the tremendous differences in people's experiences to recognize that in the modern world we are all broken, that living enmeshed in so many hierarchies means that only a very few very lucky people live their lives unscathed. Rich people can insulate themselves from some of the pain of the world that poor people endure without choice. White people can retreat into privileges that come in a white-supremacist society and never know the pain that nonwhite people face. Men can stay willfully ignorant of the routine injuries to women's bodies and spirits that come with patriarchy. Not all suffering is equal or equivalent. In oppressive systems, those on top and those on the bottom face radically different privileges and penalties, just for being who they are. As a white man in a heterosexual relationship, holding a job that pays more than a living wage for work I enjoy, living in the United States—in short, as someone near the top of the privilege pile—I am well aware of the incredible unearned advantages made available to me by virtue of my identity. I am also aware of the ways in which I am broken.

To be a person in the modern world is to be broken, to live in a world that has separated us in fundamental ways from ourselves, from others, and from the nonhuman world. In this sense we are all broken, and we all need a sense of the sacred, a place to heal. Our emotional needs bring us to church, and in church we feel. It is a place to heal.

SACRED SPACE

"Healing" has become one of the most overused and, therefore, undervalued terms in contemporary culture. What should be a sacred term reserved for one of the most powerful processes in our lives—the struggle by which we move from brokenness toward wholeness—is instead used cravenly by those claiming to be able to cure us of various physical, psychological, or spiritual ailments. Rejecting the hucksters, we also can think of healing as more than the process by which we resolve a conflict with another or within ourselves. This deeper sense of healing goes beyond what can be accomplished in a therapist's office, for example, to involve a sense of something sacred. In this sense we never fully heal, but instead strive for healing by moving toward a wholeness that we can never fully achieve in a fallen world of hierarchy. Striving to heal involves surrender—not the surrender of our power to a force outside ourselves, but rather an acceptance of the reality that we will always struggle and never reach our goal. We accept that in such a process we must turn to others for help. So that space in which we struggle must be communal, even though the process often involves solitary struggle.

My first recognition of this came that Sunday in November 2005, when I sat down after preaching. I felt good after my sermon, recognizing that it had been well received and that the congregation seemed to like me, but I also felt bad. Or, perhaps more accurately, I had a sense that the church was a place where I could feel free to feel bad, to move into a certain kind of emotional space. I didn't immediately rush to talk with people about the more personal details of my life; I didn't assume that it would be appropriate just by virtue of common membership. Rather it was the feeling of being in healing space that was important to me, a feeling I would call a recognition of the sacred. Again, experiences of the sacred are not confined to church, but church is one place we look for them. It has little to do with the building, but rather with the understanding that this space is set aside for precisely this—to go deeper into ourselves so that we may be not only more fulfilled but more present for others as well. We do this in the presence of others for ourselves, so that we can return to others closer to wholeness and more available to them.

So what is provided by the church is not just the feeling of community, in the sense of a group of others committed to our common life. The role of church is also to provide a common space in which we can be alone. We need not always engage each other; sometimes the connection is through solitary reflection in a common space. That's why the practice of praying endures, even for those of us who are not trying to communicate with a God out there. Rather, we recognize we are trying to reach each other and a deeper place in ourselves.

When I spoke the Lord's Prayer that day and felt so emotional, I was yearning for—and caught a glimpse of—that common space. And it filled a need I had that was not filled in other spaces. And in that space, I think we have the best chance to find truth.

THE CLARITY OF TRUTH

For all our minds' ability to process data and analyze patterns, the truth of the world will always appear to us to be chaos if we choose to limit ourselves to the rational. No matter how much we claim to know and pretend to control that chaos, the clarity we seek—the ability to make sense of that data and those patterns—requires that we engage our emotions as fully as possible. The first step is to avoid the trap I fell into so easily when I sat in my professor's office. After that particular meeting, I started reading about the emotions, including some of Naomi Scheman's work, in which she called for resisting

> the myth about the emotions, women's emotions in particular, that tells us they are irrational or non-rational storms. They sweep over us and are wholly personal, quite possibly hormonal . . . They don't, in any event, mean anything.[32]

Emotions mean quite a bit; they carry information. For example, when a woman has an emotional reaction to a sexist comment or a nonwhite person reacts emotionally to a racist insult, their understanding of misogyny and white supremacy is not impeded by that emotion but rather deepened. That reminds us

---

32 Naomi Scheman, "Anger and the Politics of Naming," in Sally McConnell-Ginet, Ruth Borker, and Nelly Furman, eds., *Women and Language in Literature and Society* (New York: Praeger, 1980), pp. 177–178.

there are many emotions that are felt, in some sense, collectively, and we come to understand most fully what they mean and what they tell us about the world not in purely personal form but collectively. We live in a culture that tends to privatize emotions, asking us to deal with emotional pain either in the private setting of a therapist's office or within intimate relationships with partners and/or friends. To love God with all our heart, I believe, means to recognize the collective nature of emotions, the way in which so much of what we feel—even though we experience it personally—is in fact shared. One place we can do that is church, within the communal space that should be at the heart of religion, where we can find ways to go deeper into our hearts, together. If we are to make sense of the chaos, we must acknowledge, but do our best to control, our fears; we must open our hearts as fully as possible, with awareness.

What makes us human in the most profound sense is not what we know or what we invent based on our knowledge. In the modern age, our lives are dominated by the various machines and structures we have created through the application of human reason. For the privileged, living in a world awash in high-tech goods and material comfort can lead us too easily to forget that those things do not make us who we are, they don't make us truly human. If we seek to love God—to love the mystery we call God and understand our humanity within that mystery— the clarity comes from feeling at home on what Wendell Berry has called "the human estate of grief and joy,"[33] not only knowing that this is our place in the world but feeling it as well.

One of the most powerful expressions of the clarity of that

---

33 Wendell Berry, *The Unsettling of America: Culture and Agriculture*, 3rd ed. (San Francisco: Sierra Club Books, 1996), p. 106.

truth I have felt recently is through Jim Rigby's translation of the Apostles' Creed from the original Greek:

I trust in God, universal parent, source of all power and being, And in Jesus Christ, a unique expression of God, and our guide for living;

Conceived by the spirit of love, born of Mary's pure trust, suffered under political oppression, was tortured, killed and buried,

Descending to the very depths of nonbeing; on the third day was found living again in the midst of community: perfectly at one with God, thereafter, became our standard for living and dying.

I trust in the Spirit of Life, the universality of faith, the essential unity of all who are of good will,

I believe that no mistake is final, that love does not die with the body, and the life itself is eternal.

In a series of sermons in 2007, Rigby discussed the choices he made in producing that translation, which left him with a very different text from the traditional creed. Rigby explained that while the creed is typically seen as a definitive statement of doctrine, he was interested in recovering the poetic and mystical qualities of the text. At least for me, he succeeded—what I most remember about those sermons is how our collective reading of that creed in church made me feel, especially that last sentence.

When in church we would get to that point—"I believe that no mistake is final"—I usually stopped and listened to the congregation finish without me—"that love does not die with the body, and the life itself is eternal." At that point I always found myself choking up, overwhelmed by how true that felt and how deeply I felt it. I can't offer any rational explanation for why those words touch me so deeply, nor can I explain why reading them by myself is powerful but being part of a congregation reading them affects me much more deeply. I can say only that I feel a certain power and clarity in the words, and that I am not alone. One day in church when we got to the reading of the creed, a friend nudged me and whispered, "I really like how Jim translated this, especially that last line." I whispered back that I felt the same way. "I'll tell you, the first time I read it I teared up," she said. I smiled and told her that I still find it powerful to read or hear the words read. "Me too," she said. "There's something true about it, or maybe it's what we want to be true."

The world seems as chaotic to me as ever. Each day that goes by, my sense of what I—and we—don't know is greater than the day before. And yet each day I feel a bit clearer about the truth, no matter how cruel that truth may be.

PART III

SOUL

THE CRUELTY
OF TRUTH

Because of the events after 9/11—especially the Bush administration's disastrous invasion and occupation of Iraq—many in the United States seemed to forget that for eight years President Clinton maintained a harsh economic embargo on Iraq and instituted regular low-level bombing that killed hundreds of thousands of civilians and slowly destroyed the country, a process that Bush intensified beginning in 2003.

The United States news media mostly ignored the routine death and devastation during those years, but one phase of Clinton's war on Iraq that did make the news was Operation Desert Fox, the three-day American and British bombing and missile attack in December 1998. Those of us who were part of a movement to try to end the economic embargo protested that attack, which was clearly illegal and decidedly immoral. I happened to be visiting friends in Minneapolis at that time, and after one demonstration there I found myself talking politics with Sister Rita McDonald, a well-known local peace and social justice activist.[34] As we talked, it occurred to me that she might be assuming I was a religious person, and so I told her, "Sister, just to be clear, you should know that I'm a secular person, not religious." She grabbed my arm and shook me the way a nun can, for emphasis, saying, "That's okay, boy—you've got the spirit in your soul."

I laughed, and as we kept moving I said, "Well, I'm glad for that, but I've never really understood what people mean when they talk about spirit and the soul." A man walking behind us who overheard all this leaned toward me and said with a smile, "Don't worry, neither does anyone else."

A decade later, as I ponder the command to love God with all my soul, I'm still confused.

The spiritual is usually contrasted with the material, the soul with the body. That basic distinction isn't hard to understand. But beyond that, as I read people's attempts to define, describe, delineate the concept of the soul, I find little to hold onto. Making good on the command to love God with my mind and heart is never easy, but I can grasp the idea of employing both my rational and emotional capacities in the struggle to understand the world and fulfill my obligations to self, others, and the nonhuman world. It's hard to do, but I understand what it is I'm supposed to be doing. But the soul remains a slippery concept. In various places I found the soul conceptualized as

- a conscious nonmaterial entity that survives bodily death.
- embodied spirit.
- the ultimate internal principle by which we think and feel.

---

34 Rita is one of the four McDonald sisters, all of whom had joined the Sisters of St. Joseph of Carondelet. A short film, *Four Sisters for Peace*, was made about their lives and activism. http://www.thecie.org/sisters/

- the self-aware essence unique to a particular living being.
- our inner essence.
- our immortal essence.
- the core of human will.

The official *Catechism of the Catholic Church* weighs in this way:

> In Sacred Scripture the term "soul" often refers to human life or
> the entire human person. But "soul" also refers to the innermost
> aspect of man, that which is of greatest value in him, that by
> which he is most especially in God's image: "soul" signifies the
> spiritual principle in man.[35]

Well, that really clears things up.

I'm left to conclude that no one really has much of a clue
what they mean by the concept of the soul, and that we're all
making this one up as we go along. In such a situation, I don't
hesitate to create my own definition.

ACCEPTING MYSTERY, REPAIRING BROKENNESS, AND NOT BEING AFRAID OF THE DARK

BEST GUESS #1: "Soul" is another word for mystery. Just as
"God" is a term we use for the mystery of the world around us,
"soul" is a term for the mystery within us. When we struggle to
comprehend God in the world, we are asking for help in understanding what is beyond our ability to understand about that

---

35 *Catechism of the Catholic Church*, Article 1, 363. http://www.usccb.org/
catechism/text/pt1sect2chpt1.shtml art1

world. When we struggle to comprehend the nature of the soul, we are asking for help in understanding what is beyond our ability to understand about the nature of ourselves.

So the command to love God with all our soul is the command to recognize that our inability to know all that we might want to know about the world is matched by similar mystery internally. These limits of ours may confuse and annoy us, but such is our fate, and we best get used to it.

BEST GUESS #2: "Soul" is another word for the state of being whole emotionally. We recognize we all are broken, and we seek to repair that brokenness. Even when we acknowledge that such brokenness is part of life, we name a place we want to reach where we can imagine feeling whole, and we call that the soul. We imagine a place where all the pieces of ourselves, which can feel so fragmented in the world, come together in a coherent sense of self.

So the command to love God with all our soul is the command to act in the world to bring us closer to wholeness—within ourselves, among each other, and in our place in the larger world. We will always be broken in some way, but such is our fate, and we best get used to it.

BEST GUESS #3: Soul is the place where we recognize that reason and emotion are not separate operations housed in separate parts of us, and we accept that we cannot cleanly differentiate between the two as we take in and analyze information about the world. We may talk about thinking and feeling as different processes, but they really are part of an organic, unified human engagement with the world that cannot be broken down into parts. Philosopher Sarah Hoagland puts it clearly:

> Reasoning is part of the substance, direction, and perspective of emotions just as emotions are part of the texture, substance, and

quality of reasoning. Trying to fragment them, even if at times a relief or safer, or more intense, will only fragment our abilities.[36]

Combining these three guesses as to the nature of the soul, we could produce this definition: The soul is a name for our goal of finding a way to feel truly whole and unified as we face the mystery at the core of our being and the mystery in the world, in a process that uses all of our capacities to think and feel together. We talk about our soul as a thing, as something we have—"my soul," "the human soul." In fact, the soul may be better understood as an ideal state of being that we strive to achieve. In this sense of the term, we don't really have a soul, but instead we are always struggling to be the most soulful people we can be.

When we describe someone as "having soul," we invoke a state of being in which we are authentically ourselves and honest. When we speak of "finding a soul mate," we name our yearning to not be alone in that place and with that struggle. When we refer to someone as a "good soul," we mean that we admire not just the person's surface attributes but also something deeper she or he is trying to become. All of these common usages of the term refer to the quality of coming together, within ourselves and in connection to others, conscious of the ways we can understand that world and yet always in awe of it.

We also speak of the soul as at times moving into darkness, part of a necessary process by which we come to accept that life is defined by grief as well as joy. We face the tragic nature of our lives and confront our sorrows, we come to terms with our fragmented sense of self and struggle toward wholeness, and in the end we seek a place for gentleness in a harsh world. We

---

36 Sarah Lucia Hoagland, *Lesbian Ethics: Toward New Value* (Palo Alto, CA: Institute of Lesbian Studies, 1988), p. 186.

recognize that we need help in this task, from other people but also from something beyond what we can see. We recognize that this sorrow is an inevitable part of being human, and we deny or avoid that at our own peril. As singer/songwriter (and my partner) Eliza Gilkyson has put it, "Those are lost who / try to cross through / the sorrow fields too easily."[37]

The sixteenth-century Spanish mystic St. John of the Cross used the phrase "the dark night of the soul" to describe a crisis of faith and a profound sense of loneliness that can lead to spiritual growth. While he was speaking of a relationship to God and Jesus within a Catholic tradition, the idea of a dark night speaks to a more universal experience of facing times that challenge our settled ideas about the meaning of our lives. Gilkyson used the phrase in her song "Requiem," which she wrote after the 2004 Indian Ocean tsunami, using the healing image of Mother Mary from Christianity:

> in the dark night of the soul
> bring some comfort to us all
> oh mother mary come and carry us in your embrace
> that our sorrows may be faced
> . . .
> in the dark night of the soul
> your shattered dreamers, make them whole,
> oh mother mary find us where we've fallen out of grace
> lead us to a higher place
>
> in the dark night of the soul
> our broken hearts you can make whole

---

37 Eliza Gilkyson, "He Waits for Me," *Beautiful World*, compact disc, Red House Records, 2008.

oh mother mary come and carry us in your embrace
let us see your gentle face, mary[38]

A tsunami deepens our awareness of how harshly dreams can be shattered and how broken we can feel. But the inevitability of that sorrow—the pain of shattered dreams and the constant state of brokenness—are part of everyday life. Whatever conception we have about the nature of the power beyond us in the world, attached to the word "God" or not, there are moments when we recognize there are forces in the world that are truly beyond us, that we cannot know and control. In the words of the Buddhist teacher Chögyam Trungpa: "Hope and fear cannot alter the seasons." In those moments, we seek comfort and gentleness; we realize that to get to the higher place we must go deeper inside, to what we label the soul.

THE SELLING AND SHAPING OF OUR SOULS

We often think of our souls as transcendent, but of course our souls exist—or, more usefully, our struggle for soulfulness takes place—in this world, which is structured by systems of power. Our souls (whatever definition of the term one settles on, or settles for) don't float free in some imagined world but are shaped by those systems, either in our capitulation or resistance to them. This is implicit in the phrase "selling our soul," which is usually used to mark the act of capitulation. We typically use it self-consciously, knowing that in capitulating to some aspect of that system we will receive some earthly reward that can never be

---

38 Eliza Gilkyson, "Requiem," *Paradise Hotel*, compact disc, Red House Records, 2005. http://www.elizagilkyson.com/Requiem_lyrics.htm

adequate compensation for what we surrender. This is expressed clearly in the Gospels, when Jesus tells his disciples:

[36] For what does it profit a person, to gain the whole world and forfeit life?[39]

[MARK 8:36]

In Robert Bolt's play *A Man for All Seasons*, later made into a successful film, Sir Thomas More is convicted of treason on the perjured testimony of Richard Rich, who in exchange for his capitulation to King Henry VIII is appointed attorney general for Wales. In the play, More asks one final question of Rich after noticing that the attorney general is wearing the medallion of his new position. The stage directions call for More to look into Rich's face "with pain and amusement" and say, "For Wales? Why Richard, it profits a man nothing to lose his soul for the whole world. But for Wales?"[40]

More's retort sums up the condition of the soul of the United States. Collectively, we have capitulated to both a predatory corporate capitalism that destroys as much as it creates and a predatory nation-state that violently seeks dominance around the world to make that economic system viable. We know the predictable consequence of this is not only human suffering (usually far enough away that we can avert our eyes from it if we choose) but also ecological destruction (right under our noses but still largely ignored). Collectively, then, we have lost our soul, and for things of far less value than a position in the bureaucracy of Wales. For our souls, all that most of us get are the cheap toys

---

39 In most translations, "soul" is used instead of "life."

40 Robert Bolt, *A Man for All Seasons* (New York: Vintage/Random House, 1962), p. 92.

of empire—big houses, fast cars, cheap food, nonstop spectacle entertainment, and an endless variety of numbing drugs.

But the problem is actually much more vexing. In a world dominated by such an economic and political system, the problem is not just that people sometimes choose to do bad things that hurt others or, more often, choose not to take risks to do good things because it is so easy to accept one's place in the system. Capitulations such as Richard Rich's go on every day and do real damage to innocent people in the world, of course, but such choices are relatively easy to identify and, if we choose, to resist. We see what is at stake in such choices and understand the trade-offs, even when we pretend not to recognize them. The people who sell their souls often contribute to the suffering of others, and in the long run they lose a fundamental part of themselves, which will leave them in some kind of pain and a constant struggle to numb that pain.

But more disturbing than the selling of one's soul to the system is the way in which the system shapes all our souls. To focus only on the conscious choice of Wales is to miss the real effect on our collective soul and individual souls, for every day the system in which we live molds us at a more subtle level. How is our sense of what it means to be human shaped not through choices we make consciously but by the daily demands placed on us by a system that values only profit? When that system prefers that we all become disconnected, disembodied, dysfunctional consumers, and every day works to make us into exactly that, how do we resist? What is the effect of being told relentlessly that we are rational only when we maximize self-interest, defined in the narrowest sense of material wealth? Even if we know this to be madness, how does the madness infect us when it is all around us, coming at us in more ways than we can track, contain, and reject?

If our individual souls are always drawing on a collective sense of a human soul, and the system is defining, describing, delineating the soul—our fundamental sense of what it means to be human—in ways that are designed to maximize profit, how do we resist? The process goes on, little by little, day by day, in ways we cannot see and therefore cannot fully resist.

A former colleague once brought this point home to me in a way that made a lasting impression. Returning to work after my days off, I was catching up with her and asked what she had done with her weekend. "I bought a new car," she said. I was confused because a few weeks earlier she and I had had a conversation about the pros and cons of putting a substantial amount of money into fixing the car she had been driving, and she had decided to make the repairs and keep that car. It seemed strange to make such a major investment in a car and then trade it so soon after. I asked her why. She explained, somewhat sheepishly, that her best friend and boyfriend had both been out of town over the weekend, and she got lonely. "So I went looking at cars and just bought one," she said, laughing at what she realized was an absurd decision. I laughed, too. Both of us knew it was not a funny story, but rather a profoundly sad one that said something painful not just about the state of her life but about the culture in which we all live.

My coworker knew perfectly well that it made no sense to make a major investment in repairing a car and then sell it on a whim to buy a new car on credit. She was aware that she was throwing away most of the money she had spent on those repairs and at the same time taking on new debt that would constrain future options. She had to have known that to make such a decision rashly because she felt lonely for a couple of days indicated that something was out of balance in her life, that there were unresolved questions in her head and heart about the life choices she was making. We probably laughed because neither of us wanted to cry while sitting in the office.

The point of that story is not to make fun of her or to revel in a sense of superiority, moral or otherwise. Her behavior was, admittedly, a bit over the top, even by the self-indulgent standards of the United States, but it was in some sense normal. At that time, I was approaching the age of thirty and, while I have never experienced poverty, that job was the first that afforded me a reasonably comfortable middle-class existence, with adequate income to allow me to buy nonessential goods if I wanted them. By contemporary United States standards, I was a frugal person who never had focused much on material markers of status. I drove a modest car, stocked my apartment with thrift-store furniture and garage-sale dishes, and sported a wardrobe that was far from the cutting edge of fashion. But the previous year I had bought a motorcycle that I didn't need for transportation and used only for pleasure riding. As my income increased, I could feel the pull of affluence, how easy it was to start to believe that one needs the things that one desires and then to organize one's life around getting and using those things.

My point here is not simply to criticize the overindulgence of individuals in a hyperconsuming culture, nor to suggest that capitalism created the human desire to possess material objects. Rather, the important lesson to take away is that the system of corporate capitalism does not simply structure the economy and influence politics. It affects us all, every day, and not just in the sense that advertising shapes our tastes or influences our behavior in identifiable ways. This system, which exalts consumption and relentlessly focuses on a self-indulgent materialism, gets inside of us all—it rewires our souls. When a predatory corporate capitalism absorbs nearly all the oxygen of the culture, it becomes more and more difficult to live the soulfulness we strive for.

The evidence of that can be seen in the corporate system's relationship to this "shop till you drop" mentality. The economic system relentlessly promotes the idea that consuming will make people happy—so successfully that there is now a vast literature, both scholarly and self-help, on the problem of "compulsive shopping" or "spending addiction." And when some people start to question this system, that same corporate system reacts not by trying to eliminate those who resist but by selling to them, too. There are now a variety of products we can buy to deal with the problem of buying too much. Do you need help "stopping overshopping"? Well, there just happens to be "A Comprehensive Program to Help Eliminate Compulsive Buying"—audio CD, shopping diary, and workbook, all for only $350.[41]

SOULLESSNESS AND THE DEATH OF EMPATHY

When we sell our souls in this sense, we suffer: Our capacity to feel the grief and joy in our own lives tends to atrophy, and that is to be mourned. But more important morally is that our capacity for empathy also tends to wither, and the cost of that is borne by others. When we capitulate to the demands and seductions of systems of power, we undermine our ability to imagine how other people might experience the world and, therefore, what others might be feeling, which increases the likelihood of oppressive behavior. The most dramatic examples of that come when people not only stop empathizing with others but go a step further by dehumanizing those others, making violence against them easier to commit. Human history is full of examples of that

---

41 http://www.stoppingovershopping.com/compulsive_spending.htm

process and its consequences. But recounting the most horrific stories of that dehumanization and violence is, in some sense, too easy—from a distance, almost everyone condemns such acts. The smaller case studies in the death of empathy can be more telling, if we dare see ourselves in them. I came across a vivid example of this kind of cruelty recently.

For a year I was a cofacilitator with Bernestine Singley for the Bermuda Race Relations Initiative, a government-sponsored program aimed at confronting honestly the white-supremacist past and present of that small island in the mid Atlantic. The experience, in personal and political terms, left me wondering whether 500 years of deeply entrenched white supremacy could ever be significantly reversed. One such moment came during our May 2007 visit, which in addition to the regular dialogues included a trip to Tucker's Town. For weeks before that trip, I had been hearing about Tucker's Town in Bermuda, the story of the displacement of a group of ordinary people in the 1920s to make way for an upscale resort for rich folks. It was a sad story, but just one of many sad stories in this world; I didn't expect that our trip to Tucker's Town would have any particularly dramatic effect on me. That was before I walked over the ridge of the driving range at Tucker's Point Club.

First, a little background: In Bermuda in the 1920s, businessmen were trying to restart the tourist trade that had been interrupted by World War I. Investors who wanted to build an exclusive resort for foreign tourists, especially the rapidly expanding affluent crowd from the United States, identified the Castle Harbor area on the eastern part of the island as a prime spot. The only problem was that there were dozens of families living happily there, farming and fishing, with clear title to the land. Some were willing to sell, but many had no interest in leaving their thriving community. They had family, friends, and faith in a beautiful place that allowed them to make an adequate living. Why would they want to leave?

A few more facts: The men who wanted to build the resort were white and wealthy. The resort would cater to wealthy white people. The families who lived there were black. Care to guess how it turned out? The white folks in business got the white folks in politics to pass a law to expropriate the land, the black folks got pushed out, and the resorts got built—one more place in this world where money and racism won out over justice and the interests of ordinary people. One small story in modern history, a history littered with ugly stories of power crushing people.

Singley and I went with the participants in the race dialogue to Tucker's Point, one of the two most prestigious country clubs in Tucker's Town. Singley had talked at some length with members of the Tucker's Town Historical Society who had done the important work of remembering—researching and keeping alive the history—and she realized it would be a great place to ground the reality of the island's history of white supremacy. The first stop on that day's Tucker's Town tour was the gravesite, a place the Historical Society members had identified and forced the club to restore and mark. We were told that the club had agreed to shut down the driving range while we were there, to make sure none of us would be hit by golf balls. Before we got there, I pictured the graves being off to the side of the driving range and that the closing was necessary in case a sliced shot came our way.

As we made our way from the clubhouse down to the gravesite, Bernestine and I came over the ridge, and the graves came into view. I looked down and gasped, realizing the gravesite was not off to the side but right in the middle of the driving range. I stopped to take it all in. Every day, club members and their guests were hitting golf balls onto those graves. This was a cemetery in the middle of a driving range. These were the graves of relatives of the people pushed out to make the exclusive club possible. White people were raining golf balls down on the graves of black people.

Within a few seconds, as all this came crashing into my head, I burst into tears. I turned to Singley and mumbled, "Oh my God." I started sobbing hard. I looked down at the yellow practice golf balls all around outside the walls of the gravesite and noticed there were no balls within the walls. The grounds crew must have gone in to pick up the balls on the graves, those balls that the golfers had been raining down on the graves, just before we got there. All I could say: "This is sick."

As the rest of the group made its way to the gravesite, I hung back and waited for the tears to stop. One source of the grief was knowing that the people who had relatives buried there were in pain. How must they feel looking at these golf balls? But I also was thinking about the golfers who routinely hit these balls into a cemetery. Do they even think about it?

As the crimes of humans against humanity go, this one doesn't rate as very extreme. In the richest country in the world, we routinely walk down city streets and step over homeless people sleeping, while half a world away our military pilots drop cluster bombs on civilian areas without a second thought. There are people alive today who lived through concentration camps and others who watched atomic bombs dropped on undefended cities. In comparison, a few golf balls hit into a gravesite hardly rates as an example of human depravity. But it was exactly the banality of it all that took my breath away. It was something about the ease with which we who are privileged can train ourselves not to see, the way in which a simple act of humanity that costs nothing is sometimes too much for the privileged.

The simple solution at Tucker's Point would be to move the driving range. After the displacement of people, at least give their descendants a way to honor their loved ones. At least honor the sacredness of a cemetery. We all find a way to mark the passing of those we love. We all understand funerals and memorial services, cemeteries and the scattering of ashes. It's part of being human. Societies mark births and deaths in different ways, but nowhere in this world do people routinely hit golf balls into the cemeteries of their own people, as if the graves weren't there. People don't do that to their own people. So if they do it to the dead of other people, what does it mean? It means they don't see those other people as people, as fully human. It means they value their golf game over the simple humanity of others. It means those people hitting the balls (all rich, almost all white) are saying to those people whose relatives are buried there (all black, mostly of modest means) one thing: You aren't fully human. You don't matter. We don't have to care, and we don't. We don't care enough to move a driving range. We value the act of hitting a golf ball more than the sanctity of a cemetery. More than *your* cemetery.

This means that those people hitting the golf balls have lost the capacity for empathy and, hence, have lost their own souls. To love God with all our soul, we must have a soul. Our capitulation to power and privilege must not be so extensive that we have lost touch with ourselves and with others. We must have a strong enough sense of our own humanity to recognize the humanity of others. It's difficult to imagine a world crueler than one in which we have lost that.

THE CRUELTY OF TRUTH

When I mentioned to a friend that I was writing about the soul and the cruel truths we must face, he assumed that I was focusing on our mortality, the struggle to face the inevitability of our death. I was struck once again by how uninteresting that question is to me, and how little time I have spent pondering it. When I think about the concept of the soul, it's never in the context of an afterlife but in the here and now.

Some years ago I settled on my belief about our fate after the death of our physical body. My theology on this matter, simply stated, is: We're all food for something, and food is good. We all have an important path after death, and it is the path back to the earth to enrich the soil and provide food for some other living thing, and there is no more glorious future we could imagine for ourselves. This is meant neither as false bravado nor adolescent joking. I am not suggesting that in the face of life threatening situations I have no fear; the few times I've been in situations in which I recognized that an accident could turn fatal or have been threatened with serious violence, I have been as scared as the next person. And I'm not making fun of those who believe that some aspect of our spirit or soul or essence transcends the end of our physical bodies. On questions for which there is no data available that allows us to even venture a guess, all plausible options deserve consideration.

While I don't know how I'll react when I face death and can't know what is on the other side of that moment, I can look around and observe that all living things die, and when they die the substance of their bodies returns to the land and water that gave rise to them, and that other living things draw on that sustenance. That is not a trivial observation, but in fact is one definition of the sacred, the ongoing cycle of life. As a result, my image of my death is not of a soul or spirit rising out of my body to some other plane, but of my body going back to the earth to become part of the life cycle, becoming food for other living things. The image is not just of my body going back down into the earth, but of all aspects of me becoming of the earth at a more elemental level, where I can do the work of nourishing other living things. I believe this is holy work.

So when thinking of the soul and the cruelest truths we face, instead of moving to the afterlife, I remain firmly rooted in this life and in the political analysis required to face what is to me a much more wrenching question: How do we deal with a system that attempts to rewire our souls and undermine our ability to make good on our professed values of justice and equality? How do we resist a system that can so numb us that we not only abandon those values but often fail to see the conflicts between those values and the system? Singer/songwriter Greg Brown is speaking of the future when he speculates that one day, "There'll be one corporation selling one little box / it'll do what you want and tell you what you want and cost whatever you got."[42] But it's hard not to wonder if that box is not already on sale everywhere. We should be worrying not about where our souls might travel after we die, but whether our souls can survive the world in which we live.

This cruel truth is our crucible, where we have the chance to define ourselves by how we act.

---

42 Greg Brown, "Where Is Maria?" *Further In*, Red House Records, 1996.

PART IV

STRENGTH

THE CRUCIBLE
OF TRUTH

From Jesus' first commandment, I take the task of loving one God as the need for the human family to struggle to accept the mystery of the world that is beyond us; seeking to understand it as fully as possible by using our minds, hearts, and souls; and bringing all our of resources—individually and collectively—to bear on that struggle. The final component of this effort is our strength. We must develop the will and find the energy—again, individually and collectively—to face difficult truths, no matter how painful, and then act on our analysis, no matter how hard it is to do so. Central to this endeavor is recognizing where our power lies, which requires clarity about what kind of power we will invoke.

In a culture based on hierarchy, power is most commonly viewed as the ability to force others to do what they would otherwise not do, or as the ability to do what one desires no matter what others demand. In this world, I am powerful if I can bend others to my will while remaining unbent to the will of others. Power in this sense is marked by constraints placed on us or the absence of those constraints; it's a question of being controlled or being free of control.

This plays out in many ways in our daily lives. For example, in my work as a professor at the University of Texas, administrators have some power over me, though it is largely invisible most of the time. When I go into the classroom to teach, I am doing what I enjoy and value, something I would do without being forced. Yet it also is my main source of income, and the power of my supervisors is evident when I administer exams and turn in my grade sheets at the end of the semester. If not for the ability of the institution to bar me from the classroom and/or stop paying my salary, I would not give exams nor grade students, activities I find repugnant and counter to the goals of real education. But because university officials have the power to deprive me of things I value, I do what I would otherwise not do. Those administrators have some power over me.

In that same system, I also have some power delegated to me by my supervisors. When I am in the classroom, under the current system of academic freedom, I have some power to set the direction of the course and shape the experience of students. In this sense, I have power to act in ways that I believe are appropriate, and it is the students who have to submit to my conception of what the class should be; if they don't, I have the power to assign a lower grade to them at the end of the semester, which might affect their sense of self, access to scholarship money, or future job prospects.

We all live enmeshed in complex systems that create such hierarchy and both impose power on us and allow us to exercise some power, depending on our status. The authority on which that power is based can be political, economic, cultural, theological; it can be exercised through governments, corporations, media, churches; it is executed by bureaucrats and police, owners and managers, journalists and celebrities, ministers of all kinds. Sometimes the source of the power is violence or the threat of violence; sometimes it is control over property and resources; sometimes it is the power of ideas that we come to believe, or at least accept. But there is one common feature to this kind of power: It is dead power.

POWER-OVER IN A DEAD WORLD

Whatever the arena in which it is exercised, this conception of power is about dominance and submission. Power is marked by the ability to impose or the ability to resist that imposition. This is what some have called "power-over,"[43] which assumes a zero-sum game in which individuals are always in competition for that power—someone dominates and someone submits. In such a world, one can use this kind of power with varying levels of responsibility to others, but in such a world it is inevitable that power routinely will be used unjustly. Because there is always the threat that some other person or group can grab the power, these kinds of systems will encourage people to seek always more power. This is readily evident, for example, in the emergence of the United States as the dominant power after World War II. Even though it was clear the United States could have lived relatively secure in the world with its considerable wealth

---

43 The power-over/power-with distinction is usually credited to Mary Parker Follett, a theorist, political organizer, and social activist who wrote several influential books in the first half of the twentieth century. The terms are used today in a variety of academic, political, and business settings. I first encountered this term in discussions with feminist activists. For a review, see "Feminist Perspectives on Power," *Stanford Encyclopedia of Philosophy*, October 2005. http://plato.stanford.edu/entries/feminist-power/

and extensive resources, that status was instead a source of anxiety in a power-over world, as seen in this conclusion of the State Department's Policy Planning Staff in 1947: "To seek less than preponderant power would be to opt for defeat. Preponderant power must be the object of U.S. policy."[44]

That's the logic of power-over: One either dominates or eventually is dominated. The potential of a challenge from below means that no amount of power is enough; more always must be accumulated to ward off threats. Along the way, people pursuing these goals tend to justify the concentration of power as in the best interests of all; the enlightened ones with the power tell us that they will use it benevolently in the interests not just of themselves but also those less fortunate. All of human history argues against having faith in this power seeking, with its accompanying hubris and self-delusion. But history is conveniently ignored by the powerful as they congratulate themselves on their vision and fortitude, while at the same time they work feverishly to propagandize the powerless, lest those below see the shell game for what it is and rebel.

It's tempting to say that this power-over exercised on earth is illusory, that real power rests with God or on some other plane of existence. The problem, of course, is that the suffering caused by the exercise of power-over is not illusory and does not exist at some other level. It is felt by people and other living things in the here and now. The need to challenge power-seeking, domination, and injustice is not otherworldly but of this world. Still, it is not merely rhetorical to mark that power-over is dead power. It is ultimately the power of death and also is a power

---

44 Quoted in Melvyn Leffler, *A Preponderance of Power: National Security, the Truman Administration, and the Cold War* (Stanford, CA.: Stanford University Press, 1992), pp. 18–19.

that comes only to those whose souls are dead. The poet Muriel Rukeyser expressed clearly the nature of this power and why we should reject it:

Dead power is everywhere among us—in the forest, chopping down the songs; at night in the industrial landscape, wasting and stiffening a new life; in the streets of the city, throwing away the day. We wanted something different for our people: not to find ourselves an old, reactionary republic, full of ghost-fears, the fears of death and the fears of birth. We want something else.[45]

We want something else, but our systems and institutions rarely provide it. Even the church itself, where we might assume we could find that "something else," is mired in a domination/subordination dynamic. Much Christian theology is rooted in the idea that people are so inherently evil that we must subordinate ourselves to God, and then—convenient for church officials—to a calcified dogma and doctrine propagated by the church. It shouldn't be surprising that this conception of Christianity coexists comfortably with the power-over exercised by the contemporary nation-state and corporation. These groups of elites—political, economic, religious—take for themselves the right to dominate in their arena, eyeing the other elites nervously, knowing they must collaborate with each other but always aware they also are in nervous competition in the struggle for primacy. Such is the nature of life, even for the ultraprivileged, in a power-over world.

We must give this kind of system its due: Clearly, a system

---

45 Muriel Rukeyser, quoted in Adrienne Rich, *What is Found There*, (New York: W. W. Norton, 1993), page preceding preface. Originally published in *The Life of Poetry* (New York: Current Books, 1949).

based on power-over can be productive—it can extract resources from the earth and energy from people to produce a vast array of goods and services, which brings some benefits to some people. But just as clearly, such a system can never be truly creative—it cannot create a world in which all people flourish, create new ways of understanding, or create solutions to the problems power-over inevitably generates. Such flourishing, understanding, and problem solving come not from power-over but from power-with, an understanding of power not based in assertions of independence and destructive dominance but in an embrace of interdependence and creative cooperation.

POWER-WITH IN A LIVING WORLD

In a hyperindividualized society based on capitalism's glorification of greed, it's not surprising that an adolescent conception of selfish independence would define our political and economic institutions and dominate our cultural imagination. Of course the struggle for a certain kind of independence—being free from the imposition of power-over—is not a trivial matter; we see what inhumanity is possible when people are not truly free to act as individuals, and we know that independence at the personal level matters in our lives. Yet we all know that we are not independent beings but profoundly interdependent with each other, with other organisms, and with the nonliving world. The task is to create a system that gives us freedom from the illegitimate authority that people and institutions attempt to impose on us, but recognizes our obligations to each other. One way to think through this is to imagine what a world would look like if power were not "over" but "with," if we understood that our power can be magnified in collaboration with others.

Even in the midst of a capitalist economy structured on power-over, experiments in power-with go forward, such as worker cooperatives that are owned and controlled by members. The United States Federation of Worker Cooperatives estimates that there are more than 300 such democratic workplaces in the United States, employing 3,500 people and generating about $400 million in annual revenues, mostly concentrated in the Northeast, the West Coast, and the upper Midwest. Worker cooperatives tend to create stable jobs, foster sustainable business practices, and support linkages among different segments of the community. The principles articulated by the federation capture the spirit behind, and organization of, cooperatives. voluntary and non-discriminatory open membership; control by members; equitable and democratic control of capital; commitment to education and training of members; cooperation with other cooperatives; and a commitment to sustainable community development.[46]

One exciting example of this model is Green Worker Cooperatives, which was established to incubate worker-owned and environmentally friendly cooperatives in the South Bronx. The first cooperative they launched, the ReBuilders Source, is a retail warehouse for surplus and salvaged building materials recovered from construction and demolition jobs. In the Green Worker Cooperatives' own words:

Our approach is a response to high unemployment and decades of environmental racism. We don't have the luxury to wait for

46 United States Federation of Worker Cooperatives, "About Worker Cooperatives." http://www.usworker.coop/. See also International Organization of Industrial, Artisan and Service Producers' Cooperatives, "World Declaration on Cooperative Worker Ownership," February 2004. http://www.usworker.coop/public/documents/Oslo_Declaration.pdf

new alternatives. That's why we're creating them. We believe that in order to address our environmental and economic problems we need new ways to earn a living that don't require polluting the earth or exploiting human labor.[47]

For many, it's hard to imagine working in institutions based on real cooperation because the society in which we live is structured on such a different notion. Yet if we think of experiences when we feel authentically most at home—not just our home with family, but with friends, in political groups, at church, in a community association—we typically feel powerful not because we can force people to do things or can ignore other people's needs in our decisions; we feel powerful when we come together with others to create something we couldn't have created alone.

Though it sounds paradoxical in this culture, this leads to an important insight:

We are most free when we are most bound to others.

When bonds are created under conditions of mutual respect and shared power, our freedom is deepened by such interdependence. Our strength is not sapped by these bonds but is enhanced by the emergent properties of collective human action. The individual efforts of numerous people cannot simply be added together and plugged into an equation to predict the outcome, but rather their simple actions come together in a collective result that is novel and irreducible. The most creative force does not come from a power, centralized either in one person or one institution and its bureaucracy, which imposes its

---

47 Green Worker Cooperative, "Advocating Zero Waste." http://www.greenworker.coop/

will on others and treats people as inputs whose energy can be plugged into a formula for production. The most creative force comes from distributed power that channels the contributions of many into ends that people define collectively. This goes against the cultural icon of the heroic figure, who may enlist the help of others but, in the end, draws on a power that is individual and ultimately in conflict with other power in the world. Heroic figures typically are overrated, as those who are put in that role often understand. In Brecht's play *Galileo*, the famed scientist's assistant is devastated when Galileo recants his scientific beliefs under threat from the Inquisition. Andrea confronts Galileo: "Unhappy is the land that breeds no hero." Galileo responds, "No, Andrea: Unhappy is the land that needs a hero."[48]

This notion of power-with is important not just for thinking of our interactions with other people but also for understanding our relationship to the nonhuman world. I use the term "nonhuman" instead of "nature" because to talk of humans and nature is to risk imagining that we are outside of, and separate from, nature. Instead, we should understand ourselves as part of nature, realizing that sometimes it is helpful to distinguish between the human and nonhuman elements of nature. Rather than trying to dominate and control that nonhuman world— that is, rather than seeking power-over, as humans have done[49] evermore intensely each year—we can understand ourselves more appropriately as part of that whole and recognize that our only hope is power-with.

We would profit from this approach to power because nature

---

48 Bertolt Brecht, *Galileo* (New York: Grove Press, 1940), p. 115.

49 This might be better phrased "as men have done," given the patriarchal tone of this approach to nature and science. For a review of that history, see Evelyn Fox Keller, *Reflections on Gender and Science* (New Haven, CT: Yale University Press, 1985).

is clearly far more creative than humans could ever be. Looking at my own body: Nature arranges cells to create me through processes that even the most learned biologist can never fully chart and comprehend. Looking at the universe: Nature arranges matter and energy and manages forces that even the most learned physicist must acknowledge are beyond our capacity to understand. Simple questions help focus our attention: What is more impressive, a human-made skyscraper or the complex interactions we find in a square inch of soil? What mystifies us more, the internet or the call of a bird? Nature creates at a much more profound level than humans are capable of, and we would be well-advised not to seek power over it but find power with it.[50]

One important example of this is the Land Institute and its work on Natural Systems Agriculture (NSA). While the "advances" in oil-based industrial agriculture have produced tremendous yield increases during the last century, no one has come up with a sustainable system for perpetuating that kind of agricultural productivity. Those high yields mask what Wes Jackson has called "the failure of success": Production remains high while the health of the soil continues to decline dramatically—primarily because of erosion and chemical contamination of land and water.[51] That kind of "success" guarantees the inevitable collapse of the system. The Land Institute's mission is to fashion an agriculture that will allow people, communities, and the land to prosper in sustainable fashion.

NSA investigates ways that monoculture annual grains (such as corn and wheat) can be replaced by polyculture (grown in combinations) perennial grains, attempting to mimic nature instead

---

50 See Wes Jackson, "Conceptual Revolutions: Who Needs Them and Why?" *Public Library Quarterly*, 24:3 (May 2007): 39–49.

51 Jackson, *New Roots for Agriculture*, chapter 2.

of subduing it. Jackson points out that when left alone, a natural ecosystem such as a prairie recycles materials, sponsors its own fertility, runs on contemporary sunlight, and increases biodiversity. The question NSA poses is whether agriculture can be designed to increase ecological wealth in such fashion rather than degrade it. The mission statement of the organization captures the scope of the task and the benefits of such a perspective:

> When people, land, and community are as one, all three members prosper; when they relate not as members but as competing interests, all three are exploited. By consulting Nature as the source and measure of that membership, The Land Institute seeks to develop an agriculture that will save soil from being lost or poisoned while promoting a community life at once prosperous and enduring.[52]

There is no guarantee, of course, that in the short run people who invoke power-with can persevere in the face of those employing power-over. One can pontificate about how in the long run the collaborative efforts of the collective will prove to be the better path, but as the economist John Maynard Keynes put it, in the long run we're all dead. In a system that rewards power-over, those who play that game will tend to come out on top, in the short term. The challenge is to figure out how we can, in the short term, break the hold that power-over has on the culture. This requires not just action but also analysis. One way to approach that analysis is an examination of the fundamentalisms that arise in a power-over world.

---

52 The Land Institute, "Mission Statement." http://www.landinstitute.org/

STRENGTH IN THINKING:
THE FOUR FUNDAMENTALISMS

We usually think of strength in terms of action; we draw on our strength to do things. But strength is also required in thinking, in working out the analysis we need to guide our action. It can be hard work to explore, examine, and develop an understanding of the world. It also can be difficult to face painful truths that emerge in such an endeavor. That is why fundamentalism is such an attractive way of thinking for so many—it relieves us of the need to face some of that struggle. But, in fact, fundamentalism is better described as a system of nonthought, for as Wes Jackson puts it, "Fundamentalism takes over where thought leaves off."[53] Today the United States, as a society, is suffering as a result of four key fundamentalisms. In ascending order of threat, these fundamentalisms are religious, national, economic, and technological. All share some similar characteristics, while each poses a particular threat to democracy and sustainable life on the planet.

Fundamentalism has a specific definition in early twentieth-century Protestant history as a movement to promote "The Fundamentals," but more generally the term can be used to describe any intellectual, political, or theological position that asserts an absolute certainty in the truth and/or righteousness of a belief system. Such fundamentalism leads to an inclination to want to marginalize, or in some cases eliminate, alternative ways to understand and organize the world. After all, what's the point of engaging in honest dialogue with those who believe in heretical systems that are so clearly wrong or even evil? In this sense, fundamentalism is an extreme form of hubris—overconfidence

---

53 Wes Jackson, "From the Margin," *Orion Online*, 2001.

not only in one's beliefs but also in the ability of humans to understand complex questions definitively. Fundamentalism isn't unique to religious people but is instead a feature of a certain approach to the world, rooted in mistaking limited knowledge for wisdom. That said, not all fundamentalisms pose the same danger to democracy and sustainability.

RELIGIOUS AND NATIONAL FUNDAMENTALISM

The fundamentalism that attracts the most attention is religious. In the United States, the predominant form is Christian. Elsewhere in the world, Islamic, Jewish, and Hindu fundamentalisms are attractive to some significant portion of populations, either spread across a diaspora or concentrated in one region, or both. Given all the attention focused on religious fundamentalism in recent years—and the criticism of such fundamentalism that is explicit or implicit throughout this book—I won't spend time on it here, in favor of examining other fundamentalisms loose in the world, and especially in the United States. Certainly much evil has been done in the world in the name of religion, especially the fundamentalist varieties, and we can expect more in the future.

Moving up the list, we also can see clearly the problems posed by national fundamentalism. Nationalism poses a threat everywhere but should especially concern us in the United States, where the capacity for destruction in the hands of the most powerful state in the history of the world is exacerbated by a pathological hyperpatriotism that tends to suppress internal dissent and leave many unable to hear criticism from outside. In other writing I have outlined in some detail an argument that patriotism is intellectually and morally bankrupt.[54] Given the obvious fact that a nation-state is an abstraction (lines on a map, not a naturally occurring object), assertions of patriotism (defined as love of or loyalty to a nation-state) raise a simple question: To what we are pledging our love and loyalty? How is that abstraction made real? I conclude that all the possible answers are indefensible and that instead of pledging allegiance to a nation, we should acknowledge and celebrate our connections to real people in our lives while also declaring a commitment to universal principles that are not rooted in any particular nation-state. It is a tragic mistake to offer our loyalty to arbitrary political units that have been the vehicle for such barbarism and brutality.

That principle applies across the board, but because of our power and peculiar history, a rejection of national fundamentalism is most crucial in the United States. The dominant conception of that history is captured in the phrase "the city upon a hill,"[55] the notion that the United States came into the world as the first democracy, a beacon to the world. As soon as it had the capacity to project its power abroad, the United States claimed to be the vehicle for bringing democracy to that world. These are particularly odd claims for a nation that owes its very existence to one of the most successful genocides in recorded history, the near-complete extermination of indigenous peoples to secure the land and resource base for the United States. It is odder still

---

54 Jensen, *Citizens of the Empire*, chapter 3.

55 This phrase is attributed to Puritan John Winthrop's 1630 sermon, "A Model of Christian Charity," which draws on Jesus' words in the Sermon on the Mount, "You are the light of the world. A city set on a hill cannot be hid." [Matt. 5:14] The late President Ronald Reagan was fond of describing the United States as a "shining city upon a hill," as he did in his farewell address on January 11, 1989. http://www.reaganlibrary.com/reagan/speeches/farewell.asp

when we look at the United States participation in the system of African slavery, which helped propel the United States into the industrial world, and at the enduring apartheid system—once formal and now informal—that arose from it. And it is odd to the point of bizarre in the context of imperial America's behavior in the world since it emerged as the dominant power after World War II and has attempted to destroy any challenge in the third world to United States dominance.

While all the empires that have committed great crimes—the British, French, Belgians, Japanese, Russians, and Soviets—have justified their exploitation of others by the alleged benefits brought to the people being exploited, there is no power so convinced of its own benevolence as the United States. I take the phrase from Robert Kagan's article "The Benevolent Empire,"[56] but the idea is common in the mainstream political discourse. The fact that most people in the rest of the world—especially those in Latin America, Africa, and Asia who have been the targets of this benevolence either in military or economic form—might disagree typically is ignored by those in power, who continue to assert that the United States is "the greatest nation on earth," maybe even "the greatest nation in history." At hearings for the House Select Committee on Homeland Security on July 11, 2002, Texas Republican Dick Armey described the United States as "the greatest, most free nation the world has ever known." California Democrat Nancy Pelosi countered that America is "the greatest country that ever existed on the face of the Earth." One of the requirements for being a mainstream American politician, Republican or Democrat, is the willingness to repeat these shallow, self-aggrandizing claims. This national

---

56 Robert Kagan, "The Benevolent Empire," *Foreign Policy*, Summer 1998, pp. 24–34.

fundamentalism rooted in the assumption of the benevolence of United States foreign and military policy works to trump critical inquiry. As long as a significant component of the United States public—including virtually the entire elite—accepts this national fundamentalism, the world is at risk.

ECONOMIC OR MARKET FUNDAMENTALISM

After the fall of the corrupt and inefficient Soviet system, the naturalness of capitalism is now taken to be beyond question. The dominant assumption about corporate capitalism in the United States is not simply that it is the best among competing economic systems, but that it is the only sane and rational way to organize an economy in the contemporary world. Although the financial crisis that began in 2008 has scared many people, it has not shaken that dominant assumption about the naturalness of capitalism.

There are many ways that people have defined capitalism and charted its history. In short form, capitalism is that economic system in which (1) property, including capital assets, is owned and controlled by private persons; (2) most people must rent their labor power for money wages to survive; and (3) the prices of most goods and services are allocated by markets. "Industrial capitalism," made possible by sweeping technological changes and imperial concentrations of capital, was marked by the development of the factory system and greater labor specialization. The term "finance capitalism" is often used to mark a shift to a system in which the accumulation of profits in a financial system becomes dominant over the production processes. Today in the United States, most people understand capitalism in the context of mass consumption, access to unprecedented levels of goods and services. In such a world, everything and everyone is a commodity in the market.

In contemporary market fundamentalism, also referred to as neoliberalism or the Washington Consensus, it's assumed that the most extensive use of markets possible, along with privatization of many publicly owned assets and the shrinking of public services, will unleash maximal competition and result in the greatest good—and all this is inherently just, no matter what the results.[57] If such a system creates a world in which most people live in poverty, that is taken not as evidence of a problem with market fundamentalism but as evidence that fundamentalist principles have not been imposed with sufficient vigor; it is an article of faith that the "invisible hand" of the market always provides the preferred result, no matter how awful the consequences may be for real people. Because ordinary people around the world often reject this ideology, elites take advantage of crises—either human-induced, such as a military coup, or natural, such as a tsunami—to impose the neoliberal model during a time of shock.[58]

A corresponding tenet of the market fundamentalist view is that the government should not interfere in any of this, that the appropriate role of government is to stay out of the economy. After the government bailouts that began in 2008 with the financial industry, this aspect of the ideology is particularly absurd. But it has always been a ridiculous claim, for the obvious reason that it is precisely government that establishes the rules for any economic system (currency, contract law, etc.) and decides whether

57 For a review of those results, see Mark Weisbrot, Dean Baker, and David Rosnick, "The Scorecard on Development: 25 Years of Diminished Progress" (Washington, DC: Center for Economic and Policy Research, 2005). http://www.cepr.net/documents/publications/development_2005_09.pdf

58 Naomi Klein, *The Shock Doctrine: The Rise of Disaster Capitalism* (New York: Picador, 2007).

the wealth accumulated under previous sets of rules should be redistributed or allowed to remain in the hands of those who accumulated it (recalling the quip that behind every great fortune is a great crime—such wealth is typically gained in ways immoral, illegal, or both). To argue that government should stay out of the economy merely obscures the obvious fact that without the government—that is, without rules established through some kind of collective action—there could be no economy in a complex society. The government can't stay out because it's in at the ground floor, and assertions that government intervention into markets is inherently illegitimate are silly.

But the market fundamentalists really don't want the government to sit on the sidelines; they want the government in the game on their side, ready to bail them out when things go sour. And then there's the reality of how some government programs—most notably the military and space departments—act as conduits for the transfer of public money to private corporations under the guise of "national defense" (which has nothing to do with real defense) and the "exploration of space" (which offers no tangible benefits to ordinary people). Critical examination of such programs typically focuses on the most egregious cases of corruption (such as the 2005 bribery scandal involving a defense contractor that landed California congressman Randall "Duke" Cunningham in prison) or a particularly bloated and unnecessary project (such as the F-22 "Raptor" fighter jet, a $65-billion turkey that as of 2008 had never been used in combat), leaving unasked a more fundamental question: With so many pressing human needs going unmet, why is public money being channeled into a war machine that entrenches elite power rather than creates real security and into a space program that has never been adequately justified?

And then there's the problem of market failure—the inability of private markets to provide some goods or provide other goods at the most desirable levels—of which economists are well aware. The fact that wealthy and powerful people routinely abandon their precious fundamentalist principles when it is in their interests—well, never mind that. "Pay no attention to that man behind the curtain," to the Wizards of Market Fundamentalism.

Economic fundamentalism—the worship of markets combined with steadfast denial about how the system actually operates—leads to a world in which not only are facts irrelevant to the debate, but people learn to ignore their own experience. One of those facts: There is a widening gap between rich and poor, both worldwide and within most nations. A 2005 United Nations report, aptly titled *The Inequality Predicament*, stressed:

> Ignoring inequality in the pursuit of development is perilous.
> Focusing exclusively on economic growth and income generation
> as a development strategy is ineffective, as it leads to the accu-
> mulation of wealth by a few and deepens the poverty of many;
> such an approach does not acknowledge the intergenerational
> transmission of poverty.[59]

The power of this fundamentalism can be seen in an acronym that elites try to push on us: TINA, "there is no alternative," the phrase made famous by former British prime minister Margaret Thatcher. Remember, an economic system doesn't just produce goods but produces people as well. Our experience of work shapes us. Our experience of consuming those goods shapes us. Increasingly, we are a nation of unhappy people consuming

---

59 United Nations, *Report on the World Social Situation 2005: The Inequality Predicament.*

cheap consumer goods, hoping to dull the pain of unfulfilling work. But we are told there is no alternative.

In response, we might recall a more common acronym: TGIF. Everyone in the United States knows what that means: "Thank God it's Friday." The majority of Americans don't just know what TGIF stands for—they live it and feel it. That's a way of saying that a majority of Americans do work they generally do not like and do not believe is really worth doing. That's a way of saying that we have an economy in which most people spend at least a third of their lives doing things they don't want to do and don't believe are valuable. TINA is the fundamentalist response to a TGIF world. Like all fundamentalisms, it is compelling only if we deny the complexity of the world and deny the reality of our own lives.

TECHNOLOGICAL FUNDAMENTALISM

Religious, national, and economic fundamentalisms are frightening, but they may turn out to be less dangerous than our society's technological fundamentalism.

Technological fundamentalists believe that the increasing use of evermore sophisticated high-energy, advanced technology is always a good thing and that any problems caused by the unintended consequences of such technology eventually can be remedied by more technology. Those who question such declarations are often said to be "antitechnology," which is a meaningless insult. All human beings use technology of some kind, whether stone tools or computers. An antifundamentalist position is not that all technology is bad, but that the introduction of new technology should be evaluated carefully on the basis of its effects—predictable and unpredictable—on human communities and the nonhuman world, with an understanding of the limits of our knowledge.

Our experience with unintended consequences is fairly extensive. For example, there's the case of automobiles and the burning of petroleum in internal-combustion engines, which give us the ability to travel considerable distances with a fair amount of individual autonomy. This technology also has given us traffic jams and road rage, strip malls and smog, while contributing to rapid climate change that threatens sustainable life on the planet. We haven't quite figured out how to cope with these problems, and in retrospect it might have been wise to go slower in the development of a system geared toward private, individual transportation based on the car, with more attention to potential consequences.[60]

Or how about CFCs and the ozone hole? Chlorofluorocarbons have a variety of industrial, commercial, and household applications, including in air conditioning. They were thought to be a miracle chemical when introduced in the 1930s—nontoxic, nonflammable, and nonreactive with other chemical compounds. But in the 1980s, researchers began to understand that while CFCs are stable in the troposphere, when they move to the stratosphere and are broken down by strong ultraviolet light, they release chlorine atoms that deplete the ozone layer. This unintended effect deflated the exuberance a bit. Depletion of the ozone layer means that more UV radiation reaches the Earth's surface, and overexposure to UV radiation is a cause of skin cancer, cataracts, and immune suppression.

But wait, the technological fundamentalists might argue, our experience with CFCs refutes your argument—humans got a handle on that one and banned CFCs, and now the ozone hole is

---

60 Jane Holtz Kay, *Asphalt Nation: How the Automobile Took Over America and How We Can Take It Back* (New York: Crown, 1997).

closing. True enough, but what lessons have been learned? Society didn't react to the news about CFCs by thinking about ways to step back from a developed world that has become dependent on air-conditioning, but instead looked for replacements to keep the air-conditioning running. So the reasonable question is: When will the unintended effects of the CFC replacements become visible? If not the ozone hole, what's next? There's no way to predict, but it seems reasonable to ask the question and sensible to assume the worst.

This technological fundamentalism makes it clear why Wes Jackson's call for an ignorance-based worldview is so important. If we were to step back and confront honestly the technologies we have unleashed—out of that hubris, believing our knowledge is adequate to control the consequences of our science and technology—I doubt any of us would ever get a good night's sleep. We humans have been overdriving our intellectual headlights for thousands of years, most dramatically in the twentieth century when we ventured with reckless abandon into two places where we had no business going—the atom and the cell.

On the former: The deeper we break into the energy package, the greater the risks. Building fires with sticks gathered from around the camp is relatively easy to manage, but breaking into increasingly earlier material of the universe—such as fossil fuels and, eventually, uranium—is quite a different project, more complex and far beyond our capacity to control. Likewise, manipulating plants through traditional selective breeding is local and manageable, whereas breaking into the workings of the gene—the foundational material of life—takes us into places we have no way to understand. These technological endeavors suggest that the Genesis story was prescient; our taste of the fruit of the tree of knowledge of good and evil appears to have been ill-advised, given where it has led us.

We live now in the uncomfortable position of realizing we have moved too far and too fast, outstripping our capacity to manage safely the world we have created. The answer is not some naïve return to a romanticized past, but a recognition of what we have created and a systematic evaluation to determine how to recover from our most dangerous missteps.

REDEFINING A GOOD LIFE

Central to that project is realizing that we have to learn to live with less. This is not likely to happen until we recognize that living with less is crucial, not only to ecological survival, but to long-term human fulfillment. People in the United States live with an abundance of most everything—except meaning. The people who defend the existing system most aggressively are typically either in the deepest denial, refusing to acknowledge their culture's spiritual emptiness, or else have been the privileged beneficiaries of the system's dead power and material goods. A prime example is the first President Bush, who as a reluctant participant at the 1992 Earth Summit in Rio de Janeiro declared, "The American way of life is not negotiable."[61] Translated, his statement means that hyperconsumption and unrestrained energy use is not negotiable. Nearly a decade later, his son was no more willing to challenge that declaration. When the second Bush president's press secretary was asked in May 2001 whether Americans should "correct our lifestyles" to reduce energy consumption, the answer was just as delusional: "That's a big no. The president believes that it's an American way of life, and that it should be the goal of policy

---

61 Quoted in Thomas C Fox. "Environmentalists take harsh blow," *National Catholic Reporter*, September 13, 2002, p. 5.

makers to protect the American way of life. The American way of life is a blessed one."[62]

Let's return to CFCs and air-conditioning. As someone who lives in Texas, with its miserable heat half the year, it's reasonable for me to ask, if not air-conditioning, then what? One possible response is to leave Texas, a strategy I confess that I have pondered more than once. More realistic: the "cracker house," a term used in Florida and Georgia to describe houses, built before air-conditioning was common, that utilize shade, cross-ventilation, and other building techniques to create a livable space even in the summer in the Deep South. Of course, even with all that, there are times when it's hot in a cracker house—so hot that one doesn't want to do much of anything but drink iced tea and sit on the porch. That raises a question: What's so bad about sitting on the porch drinking iced tea instead of sitting inside an air-conditioned house?

A world that steps back from high-energy, high-technology answers to all questions will no doubt be a harder world in some ways. But the way people cope without such technological "solutions" can help create and solidify human bonds. Indeed, the high-energy/high-technology world often contributes to impoverished relationships as well as the destruction of long-standing cultural practices and the information those practices transmit. It's been observed by many that when people can sit in air-conditioned comfort in front of a television, they are less likely to sit on the porch and, hence, less likely to exchange stories with neighbors. So stepping back from this fundamentalism is not simply a sacrifice but an exchange of a certain kind of comfort and easy amusement for a different set of rewards. We

---

62 Ari Fleischer, White House news briefing, May 7, 2001.

need not romanticize community life nor ignore the inequalities that structure our communities to recognize that human flourishing takes place in community and progressive social change doesn't happen when people are isolated. There's no guarantee that all conversations on that porch will be positive, but they will be conversations between real people.

Articulating this is important in a world in which people have come to believe the good life is synonymous with consumption and the ability to acquire increasingly sophisticated technology. To miss the way in which turning from the high-energy/high-technology can improve our lives leads to unthinking support for the techno-fundamentalists, such as this writer in *Wired* magazine:

> Green-minded activists failed to move the broader public not because they were wrong about the problems, but because the solutions they offered were unappealing to most people. They called for tightening belts and curbing appetites, turning down the thermostat and living lower on the food chain. They rejected technology, business, and prosperity in favor of returning to a simpler way of life. No wonder the movement got so little traction. Asking people in the world's wealthiest, most advanced societies to turn their backs on the very forces that drove such abundance is naïve at best.[63]

Naïve, perhaps, but not as naïve as the belief that unsustainable systems can be sustained indefinitely, which is at the heart of the technological fundamentalists' delusional belief system. With that writer's limited vision—which is what passes for vision

---

63 Alex Nikolai Steffen, "The Next Green Revolution," *Wired*, May 2006, p. 139–141. http://wirednews.com/wired/archive/14.05/green.html

all around this culture—it's not surprising that he advocates economic and technological fundamentalist solutions:

> With climate change hard upon us, a new green movement is taking shape, one that embraces environmentalism's concerns but rejects its worn-out answers. Technology can be a font of endlessly creative solutions. Business can be a vehicle for change. Prosperity can help us build the kind of world we want. Scientific exploration, innovative design, and cultural evolution are the most powerful tools we have. Entrepreneurial zeal and market forces, guided by sustainable policies, can propel the world into a bright green future.

The "sophisticated" thinkers ask us to ignore our experience and throw the dice, to take naïveté to new heights, to forget all we should have learned. The other path is to reject the technological fundamentalism and ask difficult questions about how we might reorder our world. Before that, we might ask an even more difficult question, not about the world, but about ourselves and what actions we are willing to take based on what we know.

STRENGTH IN ACTING:
WHAT IS A MORAL LEVEL OF CONSUMPTION?

Whatever your opinion about the pace of global warming and toxic waste accumulation, about the rate at which humans are degrading the earth's capacity to sustain life, about how long we have before our current way of living destroys the planet— one thing is beyond contention: If all the people of the world consumed at the level of the typical middle-class American, the game would be over tomorrow. The earth cannot sustain more than 6.5 billion people living as we live in the United States. Over the long term, our society is unsustainable, and in the short term our society can continue only if people in other parts of the world are consuming far less than we are.

Let's go back to the statistic I cited in the introduction: A third of the people on the planet live on less than $2 per day, while half live on less than $2.50 a day, which means that at least half the world cannot meet basic expenditures for food, clothing, shelter, health, and education necessary for a decent life. The sources of poverty, like the causes of most socio-political phenomena, are complex. But at the heart of worldwide inequality today is the continued economic domination of the underdeveloped world by the developed world. It is that system of domination that allows us to consume as we do, and it is that system that helps keep the poor of the world poor.

This kind of realization is not confined to "radical environmentalists" or "leftist revolutionaries." Consider the judgment of James Wolfensohn near the end of his term as president of the World Bank:

It is time to take a cold, hard look at the future. Our planet is not balanced. Too few control too much, and many have too little to hope for. Too much turmoil, too many wars, too much suffering. The demographics of the future speak to a growing imbalance of people, resources, and the environment. If we act together now, we can change the world for the better. If we do not, we shall leave greater and more intractable problems for our children.[64]

---

64 James D. Wolfensohn, "A New Global Balance: The Challenge of Leadership," address to the Board of Governors of the World Bank Group, September 23, 2003. http://siteresources.worldbank.org/NEWS/Resources/jdwsp-092303.pdf

I have no idea how serious people such as Wolfensohn are about supporting the change necessary to address these issues, though I'm skeptical. Whatever the case, at that meeting he was polite enough not to mention to the privileged attendees that anyone serious about our ecological future and global justice has to face this question: What is a morally defensible level of consumption in such a world?

TAKING THE QUESTION SERIOUSLY

Many people avoid the question by arguing that the key to overcoming those threats and disparities is political change, not lifestyle changes by individuals. That's certainly true; large-scale economic and political changes to overcome the problems inherent in capitalism and nation-states are required. In a power-over world, changes made by well-meaning individuals within the existing system can never be enough to change our overall trajectory. But that doesn't obscure the need for people to address the question at the personal level, for two reasons.

First, precisely because the ecological problems require large-scale, global solutions, people in the United States have to reduce their consumption. Why should anyone in the developing world take seriously any claims about the need for environmental regulation made by people in the industrial world? If we in the developed world show so little interest in curbing our own ravenously destructive habits, what standing do we have to preach to others? How can meaningful international solutions be reached when the industrial world shows so little interest in such change?

Second, if we are serious about meaningful change, political movements and personal choices cannot be separated. Our willingness and ability to work on the big-picture politics flow in part from our personal connection to the question. On any issue, we become more effective political organizers as our commitment and understanding deepen. On ecological questions, that deepening comes in part with honest self-assessment about our own life choices and willingness to act.

An analogy to the struggle for racial justice is helpful. In the 1950s in the United States, it certainly was true that no serious progress on the problem of racism would be possible without abolishing Jim Crow laws and providing meaningful guarantees of voting rights for nonwhite people. But did that mean that antiracist white people would have been justified to ignore the ways in which they themselves engaged in racist behavior, perhaps unconscious and subtle, in their personal lives, until those political changes were in place? Would we have accepted from politically active white people the claim that until the Voting Rights and Civil Rights Acts were passed, personal behavior didn't matter? Or that once those laws were passed, that's all that white people need worry about? Of course not. We would have pointed out that a real commitment to racial justice meant—and still means—that white people must not only pursue political change at the societal level but also be accountable, engage in self-criticism, and commit to changing their attitudes and behavior. In such arenas, no one suggests it is acceptable to ignore accountability for personal behavior while pursuing political goals.

So we return to the question: What is a morally defensible level of consumption?

DETERMINING A DIRECTION,
NOT DICTATING BEHAVIOR

The answer can't be that until there is justice and equity in the world, we should all consume at the level of the poorest on the planet. The poorest in the world live in misery and starve, and no one can be expected to choose a life of such deprivation. Once we accept that our individual levels of consumption do matter, we have to recognize that in a complex world there can be no easy, bright-line answer to this question. But that doesn't mean we have nothing to say about the search for answers. Instead, we can look to common ethical principles for guidance. One of those principles is the assertion that we should treat others as we would like to be treated, often called the Golden Rule or the ethic of reciprocity, a principle that shows up often in human thought, both in religious and secular teachings.[65] In Christianity, Jesus phrased it this way in the Sermon on the Mount:

> [12] So whatever you wish that someone would do to you, do so to them; for this is the law and the prophets.
>
> [MATT. 7:12]

One of the best-known stories about the great Jewish scholar Hillel from the first century BCE concerns a man who challenged him to "teach me the whole Torah while I stand on one foot." Hillel's response: "What is hateful to you, do not do to your neighbor. That is the whole Torah, while the rest is the commentary thereof; go and learn it."[66]

---

65 For a summary, see "Shared Belief in the Golden Rule." http://www.religioustolerance.org/reciproc.htm

66 Talmud, tracate Shabbat 31a. http://www.come-and-hear.com/

This is echoed in the repeated biblical command, in the Old as well as the New Testament, to "love thy neighbor as thyself." [Lev. 19:18] In Islam, one of the Prophet Muhammad's central teachings was, "None of you truly believes until he loves for his brother what he loves for himself."[67] In secular Western philosophy, Kant's categorical imperative is a touchstone: "Act only according to that maxim whereby you can at the same time will that it should become a universal law."[68]

Such a general principle does not dispose of all ethical questions, of course, but it provides a starting point for working through questions involving our use of resources: Consume at a level that could be generalized to all people. That is, the morally acceptable level of consumption is one that, if all people in the world lived at that level, would allow for sustainable life on the planet. In this context, "sustainable" means a system that would not exhaust the finite resources of the planet necessary for the survival of human and nonhuman life, and would not generate pollution and contamination at levels that make the planet unlivable. The term "sustainable development" came into vogue after it was used in the 1987 report of the World Commission on Environment and Development, known as the Brundtland Commission, which defined it simply as development that "seeks to meet the needs and aspirations of the present without compromising the ability to meet those of the future."[69]

---

67 Yahya ibn Sharaf al-Nawawi, *Al-Nawawi's Forty Hadith* (Cambridge, UK: Islamic Texts Society, 1997), Hadith 13.

68 Immanuel Kant, *Grounding for the Metaphysics of Morals,* 3rd ed. (Indianapolis: Hackett, 1993), p. 30.

69 *Our Common Future: Report of the World Commission on Environment and Development,* United Nations, 1987. http://www.un-documents.net/wced-ocf.htm Also published as *Our Common Future* (New York: Oxford University Press, 1987).

Obviously, the sustainable level of consumption depends on the size of the human population. Projections have suggested that the current world population of more than 6.5 billion will rise in the near future, perhaps as high as 10 billion by 2100, though the speed of ecological collapse makes it unlikely the population will ever reach that size. But for purposes of this question, precision is not required on either issue. Instead of seeking a definitive answer, our goal should be to assess where we stand today and determine the direction in which we must move, with some sense of the urgency of the task. We can assume the population will continue to grow in the short term and that whatever advances in technology lie before us won't solve all our problems. Given that, what we can say with great confidence is that all the people of the world cannot live at the level of Bill Gates or Donald Trump. A world of 6.5 billion Bills and Dons is not sustainable.

Those of us who aren't Bill or Don may at first find that reassuring; it's easy to focus on the wealthiest or most outrageous people and claim that they're the problem. It's been obvious for years that a typical middle-class American lifestyle also is not generalizable to the whole world. A few years ago Klaus Toepfer, head of the United Nations Environment Program, made the point that the Chinese government's aim to drastically improve the general standard of living can only occur if developed nations radically change their consumption habits to free up scarce resources for the world's poor. The Chinese nutrition goal, by which each citizen would be able to eat 200 eggs per year, would require 1.3 billion chickens. Feeding these chickens would require more grain per year than is grown in the entire continent of Australia—current patterns of agriculture and consumption would not be able to sustain such growth. If China had the same density of private cars as a developed country such as Germany, Toepfer said, it would have to produce 650 million vehicles, which the world's supply of metal and oil would be unable to sustain.[70]

So if we were to apply a Golden Rule of consumption—to consume at a level that would allow people worldwide to live a decent life consistent with long-term sustainability—it seems we would have to eat lower on the food chain and get rid of some of our cars. Actually, lots of our cars, and not just the SUVs. Again, it's easy to point a judgmental finger at the most wasteful vehicles on the road, but the real problem is the number of individually owned and operated vehicles out there. The owner of a fuel-efficient small car is implicated in this right along with the driver of the gas-hog.

So should everyone who owns a car stop driving? That certainly would improve the health of the planet, but it's not feasible immediately in a culture designed around individual car travel. Many people live in circumstances that make it impossible to maintain family, work, and social commitments without a car. Larger-scale change is necessary—most obviously the development of mass transit and the redesigning of cities to make them less auto-dependent. But that doesn't mean that as we work for those changes, there is nothing we can do as individuals. Here's a short list:

- Do not buy an auto if it is feasible.
- If one has to use an auto, create a car cooperative with others to share a vehicle.
- In a family unit, maintain the fewest vehicles possible.
- Buy the smallest and most fuel-efficient car possible.

---

70 Jonathan Watts and Steven Morris, "On the Chinese menu: 260 billion eggs and the world's entire catch of fish," *The Guardian*, July 18, 2003, p. 11.

- Use a car only when necessary, walking, biking, or taking public transportation whenever possible.
- Live as locally as possible, reducing the need for travel when feasible.

People are not morally obligated to spend all their time pondering and taking action to lower consumption. We do not live under conditions of our own individual making, and if we want to participate in the culture in a way that allows us to be politically effective, then we will never be able to claim a position of purity. The question we should ask is not, "Have you met *the* standard?" set down by some arbitrary authority, but instead, "Are you willing to confront the problem and make a good-faith attempt to move in the right direction?"

If anyone doubts that this direction must be toward far less consumption, visit the website maintained by Redefining Progress, a think tank working on sustainability and justice issues, and run through the www.myfootprint.org/ survey. Using the concept of the "ecological footprint"—the portion of the natural world that goes toward supporting one's lifestyle—the quiz graphically illustrates just how far most of us are from a just and sustainable level.[71] The reality is that, even in progressive circles where people are generally aware of the severity of the problem, many people have not taken these questions seriously. As "sacrifices" go, that simple list of actions concerning cars is trivial, yet I know many people who think of themselves as politically progressive but have not considered any of those options (perhaps beyond looking at the gas mileage figures when they buy a car). In my own life, I can see how hard it has been to maintain some

---

71 For more detail on the concept of the footprint, see http://www.rprogress. org/ecological_footprint/about_ecological_footprint.htm

of these commitments over time, especially in the absence of a well-developed alternative system in which to ground myself.

Progressive politics is always a process of destruction and creation. We argue that certain systems (patriarchy and white supremacy, capitalism and imperialism) have to be destroyed, while at the same time we struggle to articulate and create the alternatives. In that process, each of us will have different contributions to make, depending on background, temperament, circumstance, and constantly changing contingencies. Some people try to contribute by creating viable alternatives to a high-energy, high-consumption life. Others who are engaged in traditional political organizing may see these kinds of day-to-day choices as less important. But we all need to confront the choices. Humans have well-developed rationalization skills; we are gifted at finding ways of convincing ourselves of the irrefutable truth of what we want to believe. Those of us actively engaged with movements for social justice have a responsibility to resist that.

SEARCHING FOR ANSWERS, NOT PREACHING TO OTHERS

No matter how many times I emphasize that I am not arguing that there is a magic formula we can use to set an appropriate level of consumption, some will assert that is really my goal. Often people tell me, "Oh, you just think everyone should live like you do." That is not my contention, if for no other reason than that I have not achieved a level of consumption that comes close to meeting this Golden Rule standard.

One possible motivation behind a seemingly deliberate misreading is fear. As members of an affluent culture, the vast majority of us have become used to living with the material comforts of that affluence, at whatever level we live, and we typically like it. In many cases, we have become lazy, which I certainly can see in my own life. Knowing that the affluence is based on the unsustainable exploitation of the earth's resources and the unjust exploitation of vulnerable people in other parts of the world as well as less privileged classes at home can be difficult to live with. One coping mechanism is to ignore it. For the political reasons already outlined, I think that is a bad choice.

But there also is a personal cost to ignoring these difficult issues. It is my experience that when I have wrestled with these kinds of questions (such as whether to become vegetarian, for both moral and ecological reasons; or whether to give up my car; or in general whether I should reduce my participation in the mall-based culture of consumption), I have benefited immensely, both from the process of coming to a decision and the ramifications of the decision. I discovered that I like life as a vegetarian better than as a meat-eater. I found I was a happier and healthier person when I routinely rode a bicycle to work. I felt liberated by not buying things that people all around me clamor to buy.

But those decisions don't get me off the hook. Although I don't eat meat, I still eat dairy products, and I struggle daily with that decision; the honorable example set by a friend who is vegan reminds me of the question. Although I was able for many years to live without a car, a change in my personal life that led to a home further from work means I now commute in a car almost daily; a friend who walks virtually everywhere reminds me of how I fall short in this area. Although I stay away from the mall, I still eat out (a wasteful way to eat, given the way in which food is prepared and discarded in contemporary restaurants) more than is necessary; another friend who grows and cooks much of his own food reminds me of that failure of mine.

I could produce a long list of my own choices that create such conflict in me every day, and along with that, a list of people I know who do better than I in the struggle to consume less. Their examples force me to face my own shortcomings, and for that I'm grateful; that discomfort is what pushes me to struggle with these issues and leads me to change.

At some point, the entire culture will have to face this. For theologically and politically progressive people, it is crucial that we not shy away from those questions. There need be no imposition of "right answers"; what is needed is an honest conversation grounded in a willingness to engage in self-criticism and be accountable to others. Such conversations will often be difficult and sometimes quite painful—as are conversations, if they are to be true to antiracist principles, about how well white people are living; or, true to feminist principles, about how well men are living. The difficulty does not give us the right to ignore the issues, though that is a common response.

It's also an understandable response. After reading an article of mine about the American empire, a woman wrote to me and said that she could see the importance of the underlying question about our consumption. She asked me a simple question: If I want to be part of a movement for global justice, do I have to give up my house? By the tone and content of her email, I assumed she was a middle- or upper-middle-class person with a comfortable house that was bigger than she needed, a house that wouldn't meet the Golden Rule test. To be part of the movement against United States imperialism and for global justice, do folks have to give up these houses?

The answer is yes and no. Eventually, yes, because such houses simply won't be feasible in the scaled-down world that is coming. But in the short term, my answer is no. There is much political work to be done, and running out today to sell off the bigger-than-needed house likely isn't the answer. But one has to acknowledge that if there is to be global justice, we can't live in these big houses indefinitely. If we live in a small house or an apartment, we aren't off the hook. We all are implicated. We all have to struggle. It won't be easy for any of us. It can be hard even to imagine how we as a species are going to find our way out of this mess.

THE CRUCIBLE OF TRUTH

Our path in dealing with the truth is to struggle with the apparent chaos, come to whatever clarity is available to us, and then face the cruelty such a process reveals. But the crucible, the test of our capacity to face the truth, comes in the steps we take at that point. Can we move forward, even when we recognize we may face insurmountable obstacles? Can we work for justice and sustainability within a dead culture?

For many years I said in public talks that we live in a "dying culture," but I have abandoned that phrase. The dominant culture in the United States—hypernationalist ethnocentrism and a predatory corporate capitalism shaped by patriarchy and white supremacy, playing out within a broader human assault on the planetary ecosystem—is not dying. It is already dead. Of course the United States government and United States–based corporations continue to wield incredible power at home and around the world, and it may seem odd to refer to a society that can impose its will on so much of the world as a dead culture. Sick, maybe even dying, certainly in the last throes of imperial power—but dead? Yes, and the distinction in phrasing makes a difference.

Rather than saving the dominant culture, our task is not only to let it pass from the scene but also to hasten that transition. Jesus recognized, in his own time, that a radical departure from the old was necessary. When a disciple agreed to follow him but asked that he first be permitted to go and bury his own father, Jesus said to him, "Follow me, and leave the dead to bury their own dead." [Matt. 8:21–22][72]

It is time for us to stop trying to revive our dead culture, to stop believing that the nation-state and capitalism—born in, and still infected by, patriarchy and white supremacy—can be the basis for a just and sustainable future. It is time to go to a deeper level. Even with the economic and military setbacks of recent years, many in the United States hold on tightly to a delusional triumphalism—a belief that the United States is the ultimate fulfillment of human promise, that shining city upon the hill, a beacon to the world. The faith we need must give us strength to recognize we live in a dead culture and to speak this harsh truth. Beyond that, it must allow us, first, to be decent to one another despite our knowledge that being heartless will be rewarded. Second, it must embolden us to confront systems that will be intensely resistant to change and will reward those who refuse to acknowledge the urgent need for change. Third, our faith must empower us to maintain these personal and political commitments with no guarantee that we can transcend and survive this dead culture.

The ultimate test of our strength is whether we can recognize not only that we live in a dead culture but also that there may be no way out. It's true that throughout history cultures have died, empires have fallen, societies have been replaced by challengers. Through all that, the world survived. But consider the unprecedented destructive capacity of the United States military, the entrenched pathology embedded in our psyches through capitalism, the ecological damage already done, and the further damage

---

72 In a slightly different rendition, Jesus says, "Leave the dead to bury their own dead; but as for you, go and proclaim the kingdom of God." [Luke 9:60]

likely to occur during a collapse—it's no longer clear that by the time the United States empire collapses, the world will survive in anything like the form we know it. And as this future unfolds, we will have to cope with the delusions (both of grandeur and victimization) that power and affluence tend to produce in elites and the general public, which will undermine the clear thinking that will be so desperately needed.

The ultimate test of our strength is whether we would be able to persevere in the quest for sustainability and justice even if we had good reasons to believe that both projects would ultimately fail. We can't know for sure, but can we live with that possibility? Can we ponder that and yet still commit ourselves to loving action toward others and the nonhuman world?

Said differently: What if our species is an evolutionary dead end? What if those adaptations that produced our incredible evolutionary success—our ability to understand certain aspects of how the world works and manipulate that world to our short-term advantage—are the very qualities that guarantee we will destroy ourselves and possibly the world? What if that which has allowed us to dominate will be that which in the end destroys us? What if humanity's story is a dramatic tragedy in the classical sense, a tale in which the seeds of the protagonist's destruction are to be found within, and the play is the unfolding of the inevitable fall?

No one can know for sure, of course.[73] But what if? Do we have the strength to ponder that? In a let's-roll-up-our-sleeves-and-get-to-work culture, what if we were to roll up our sleeves forever and still not be able to get the job done? Most people would say we demonstrate our strength when we tackle such jobs with a can-do

---

73 For a vision of the Earth post-human, see Alan Weisman, *The World Without Us* (New York: Picador, 2008).

attitude. A demonstration of greater strength—maybe the greatest strength we can imagine—is to take on those jobs with an understanding not only that failure is possible but that it may be likely. This goes against the grain in a culture that assumes that success is inevitable. Lewis Killian described this outlook in the context of his own discipline, when looking at white supremacy in the 1960s:

> The sociologist, no matter how gloomy his predictions, is inclined to end his discourse with recommendations for avoiding catastrophe. There are times, however, when his task becomes that of describing the situation as it appears without the consolation of a desirable alternative. There is no requirement in social science that the prognosis must always be favorable; there may be social ills for which there is no cure.[74]

Nor is there a requirement in theology or politics that the prognosis always be favorable. There may be not only specific social ills for which there is no cure—it may be that we humans are just smart enough to get into trouble on all fronts but never quite smart enough to get ourselves out. What if the tragedy of human intelligence is that we are bound to create complex problems for which there are no simple solutions?

The world's scientists are speaking of these questions. James Lovelock, a fellow of the Royal Society whose work led to the detection of the widespread presence of CFCs in the atmosphere, is most famous for his "Gaia hypothesis," which understands both the living and nonliving parts of the earth as a complex system that can be thought of as a single organism. He suggests that we face these stark realities immediately:

---

74 Lewis M. Killian, *The Impossible Revolution? Black Power and the American Dream* (New York: Random House, 1968), p. xv.

The great party of the twentieth century is coming to an end, and unless we now start preparing our survival kit we will soon be just another species eking out an existence in the few remaining habitable regions . . . We should be the heart and mind of the Earth, not its malady. So let us be brave and cease thinking of human needs and rights alone and see that we have harmed the living Earth and need to make our peace with Gaia.[75]

If we are truly strong—if we love God with all our strength—we must face these questions. Strength is exhibited not by manufacturing a sense of hope that ignores reality but by facing up, while not succumbing, to a situation that may be hopeless. It doesn't mean hope is unavailable to us, but that we have to find honestly what Albert Camus called a "stubborn hope":

Tomorrow the world may burst into fragments. In that threat hanging over our heads there is a lesson of truth. As we face such a future, hierarchies, titles, honors are reduced to what they are in reality: a passing puff of smoke. And the only certainty left to us is that of naked suffering, common to all, intermingling its roots with those of a stubborn hope.[76]

If we are to claim a stubborn hope, we must come to it honestly and act from it with integrity. Historically, that kind of hope has been spoken by prophets.

---

75 James Lovelock, *The Revenge of Gaia: Earth's Climate Crisis and the Fate of Humanity* (New York: Basic, 2006), p. xiv.

76 Albert Camus, "The Wager of Our Generation," in *Resistance, Rebellion, and Death*, (New York: Vintage, 1960), pp. 239–240.

OUR
CHALLENGE

PROPHETIC
VOICES

It may be that people always want to believe they live at the most important time in history, that their moment is the decisive moment. But even factoring in this tendency toward a collective sense of self-importance, it is difficult to ignore that the multiple crises we face today—economic, political, cultural, and, most crucially, ecological—have the potential to make impossible ongoing life on the scale we know it today. Even though predictions about the specifics of the trajectory are beyond our capabilities, we can know—if we choose to know—that we must solve problems for which there are no apparent solutions and face "questions that go beyond the available answers," to borrow Wes Jackson's phrase.[77] These threats have been building for the past 10,000 years, intensifying in the past two centuries to levels that only the foolhardy would ignore. The bills for the two most destructive revolutions in human history—the

---

77 Wes Jackson, "Toward an Ignorance-Based Worldview," *The Land Report*, Spring 2005, pp. 14–16.

agricultural and industrial revolutions—are coming due, sooner than we think.[78]

Never before in this world have we had such a need for strong, principled, charismatic leadership. In the United States, where such leadership is most desperately needed at this crucial moment, the old guard in politics has failed and the younger politicians taking power offer no indication they are up to the task. We can look around the national scene—whether in politics, business, religion, or intellectual life—and see that no one measures up.

Thank goodness for that.

WE ARE ALL PROPHETS NOW

It would be seductive, as we stand at the edge of these cascading crises, to look for leaders. But where would they lead us? How would they answer the unanswerable questions and solve the unsolvable problems? Better to recognize that we are at a moment when leaders cannot help us, because we need to go deeper than leadership can take us. Perhaps there are no honestly inspiring figures on the scene—and by honest, I mean those willing to tell the truth about the nature of the systems in which we live—because those kind of authentic leaders know that we are heading into new territory for which old models of movements and politics are insufficient. Rather than trying to claim a place at the front of the parade, they are struggling to understand the direction we should be moving, just like the rest of us.

When traditional political and/or theological leadership fails,

---

78 See my interview with Wes Jackson, "Where Agriculture Meets Empire," *Alternet*, July 1, 2003. http://www.alternet.org/environment/16306/

it's tempting to want to turn to a prophet. But that too would be a mistake. This is a moment that cries out not for a prophet but for prophets. It is time to recognize that we all must strive to be prophets now. It is time for each of us to take responsibility for speaking in the prophetic voice. I don't mean this in the shallow sense of the term "prophecy," claiming to be able to see the future. The complexity of these crises makes any claim to predict the details of what lies ahead absurd. All we can say is that, absent a radical change in our relationship to each other and in the nonhuman world, we're in for a rough ride in the coming decades. Though the consequences of that ride are likely to be more overwhelming than anything humans have faced, certainly people at other crucial historical moments have faced crises without clear paths or knowledge of the outcome. A twenty-five-year-old Karl Marx wrote about this in 1843:

> The internal difficulties seem to be almost greater than the external obstacles. For although no doubt exists on the question of "Whence," all the greater confusion prevails on the question of "Whither." Not only has a state of general anarchy set in among the reformers, but everyone will have to admit to himself that he has no exact idea what the future ought to be. On the other hand, it is precisely the advantage of the new trend that we do not dogmatically anticipate the world, but only want to find the new world through criticism of the old one. Hitherto philosophers have had the solution of all riddles lying in their writing-desks, and the stupid, exoteric world had only to open its mouth for the roast pigeons of absolute knowledge to fly into it.[79]

---

79 Karl Marx, letter to Arnold Ruge, September 1843. http://www.marxists. org/archive/marx/works/1843/letters/43_09.htm

We should understand the prophetic as the calling out of injustice, the willingness not only to confront the abuses of the powerful but to acknowledge our own complicity. To speak prophetically requires us first to see honestly—both how our world is structured by illegitimate authority that causes suffering beyond the telling, and how we who live in the privileged parts of the world are implicated in that suffering. In that same letter, Marx went on to discuss the need for this kind of "ruthless criticism":

> But, if constructing the future and settling everything for all times are not our affair, it is all the more clear what we have to accomplish at present: I am referring to ruthless criticism of all that exists, ruthless both in the sense of not being afraid of the results it arrives at and in the sense of being just as little afraid of conflict with the powers that be.

To speak prophetically is to refuse to shrink from what we discover about the injustice of the world. It is to name the wars of empire as unjust; to name an economic system that leaves half the world in abject poverty as unjust; to name the dominance of men, of heterosexuals, of white people as unjust. And it is to name the human destruction of Creation as our most profound failure in our time on this planet. At the same time, to speak prophetically is to refuse to shrink from our own place in these systems. We must confront the powers that be and ourselves.

In the Christian and Jewish traditions, the Old Testament offers us many models—Amos and Hosea, Jeremiah and Isaiah—men who rejected the pursuit of wealth or power and argued for the centrality of kindness and justice. The prophets condemned corrupt leaders but also called out all those privileged people in society who had turned from the demands of justice, which the faith makes central to human life. In his analysis of these prophets, the scholar and activist Rabbi Abraham Joshua Heschel concluded:

> Above all, the prophets remind us of the moral state of a people: Few are guilty, but all are responsible. If we admit that the individual is in some measure conditioned or affected by the spirit of society, an individual's crime discloses society's corruption. In a community not indifferent to suffering, uncompromisingly impatient with cruelty and falsehood, continually concerned for God and every man, crime would be infrequent rather than common.[80]

To speak prophetically, then, is not to ponder how the world came to be or speculate about where we're going when we leave this world. The prophets were focused on the injustice of the moment—in other words, on sin. If we want to speak prophetically today, we need to think about that concept.

UNDERSTANDING SIN

In a world in which so many decent people have been psychologically and theologically abused by being called "sinner," talking of sin is not a simple task. For example, any lesbian or gay man who has been on the receiving end of hateful tirades about sin knows how the term can be used to injure deliberately, often by people afraid to face their own internal struggles and/or unwilling to think for themselves. Often the people who enjoy citing the biblical recognition that we are all sinners "[22] the

---

80 Abraham J. Heschel, *The Prophets* (New York: HarperCollins, 2001/1962), p. 19.

righteousness of God through faith in Jesus Christ for all who believe. For there is no distinction; [23] since all have sinned and fall short of the glory of God, [ROM. 3:22–23]"—are the very same people who take delight in condemning others for their sins (real or imagined), despite the equally clear command that we avoid that kind of accusatory judgment:

> [1] Judge not, that you be not judged. [2] For with the judgment you pronounce you will be judged, and the measure you give will be the measure you get. [3] Why do you see the speck that is in another's eye, but do not notice the log that is in your own eye? [4] Or how can you say to another, 'Let me take the speck out of your eye,' when there is the log in your own eye? [5] You hypocrite, first take the log out of your own eye, and then you will see clearly to take the speck out of another's eye.
>
> [MATT. 7:1–5]

So we must be careful in speaking of sin, both to avoid injuring others because of our unexamined prejudices and to check our own tendency toward self-congratulation. But we shouldn't give up on the concept of sin, for we are in fact all sinners—we all do things in our lives that fall short of the principles on which we claim to base our lives. Everyone I know has at some point lied to avoid accountability, failed to offer help to someone in need, taken more than a fair share of the bounty of the earth. Indeed, we have all sinned.

Yet we also know that all sins are not equal, that the failings of some people are dramatically more serious and costly to others. The fact that we all fall short of perfection does not mean we all fall equally short on equally important criteria. We cannot help but make such judgments if we are to be responsible for the collective health of the community and the safety of individuals in it. This is obvious when individuals commit overt acts of violence against others, but no less important in what might appear to be more complex cases. Just as we must judge a rapist or a murderer, we also must judge a doctor who has sex with a patient or a company that dumps toxins into the water. Each action may be explained away with claims of confusion or willed ignorance, but each is an abuse of power that can injure. Even if that particular patient did not feel abused by the relationship, allowing doctors to use their power over patients for self-gratification will routinely cause harm. Even if that particular dumping of toxins caused no direct harm, allowing companies seeking profits to cut corners will routinely cause harm. Both these actions are unjust and unacceptable, and developing the insight to recognize that is crucial. If we are to honor the call to humility and live up to our own moral standards, with integrity, we must deepen out understanding of sin and its causes.

CREATED AND COLLECTIVE, NOT ORIGINAL AND INDIVIDUAL

For Christians, sin traditionally has been marked as original and individual—we are born with it, and we can deal with it through an individual profession of faith. In some sense, of course, sin is obviously original; at some point in our lives, we all do things that violate our own principles, which is another way of saying that we are all born with the capacity to sin, that it is a part of the human psychological makeup. Equally obvious is that even though we live interdependently and our actions are conditioned by how we are socialized, we are distinct moral agents, and we make choices. Responsibility for those choices must in part be ours as individuals.

This conception of sin has relevance in our day-to-day efforts to become more decent people in this fragile world. We can see that much of this individual sin comes from the temptation to live in excess, from our inability at times to control normal aspects of being human. When we examine the so-called seven deadly sins (lust, gluttony, greed, sloth, wrath, envy, pride), I doubt most of us imagine the answer lies in eliminating the source of those sins—sexual desire, appreciation of food, a pleasure in material objects, enjoyment of leisure, the capacity for anger, any sense of competition with others, and satisfaction in one's achievements. The trick is finding the appropriate level for these aspects of our lives, which is rarely easy.

But at this moment in history, it is more crucial to focus on the sins we commit that are created, not original, and solutions that are collective, not individual. These sins, which do much greater damage, are the result of—we might say, created by-political, economic, and social systems. Those systems create war and poverty, discrimination and oppression, not simply through the freely chosen actions of individuals but because of the nature of these systems of empire and capitalism, rooted in white supremacy and patriarchy. Humans' ordinary capacity to sin is intensified, reaching a different order of magnitude, and responsibility for the resulting sins is shared.

As I write this, the Iraq war drags into its sixth year, with hundreds of thousands of dead, a country devastated, a region destabilized, and the world put at greater risk as a result of an illegal invasion based on lies designed to cover up the United States' imperialist goals. Who bears responsibility for this sin? Certainly the civilian leaders, Republicans and Democrats alike, who engineered or endorsed the war, pretending that wars for dominance are really intended to protect people. Certainly the military officials who carried out the plans, crafting strategies that they knew would kill large numbers of civilians. Their sins are clear.

But what of the people who profit from war and are so quick to support it, the weapons-makers and the security contractors and all the rest? And what of the politicians who did not support the war but stood by in cowardly silence rather than risk alienating pro-war constituents? What of the journalists who damped down their allegedly skeptical instincts and beat the drums of war? What of the vast majority of the population that sat back and watched it all on television rather than taking political action? And, if we are to be ruthlessly critical, what of the antiwar movement (of which I consider myself a part) that never managed to find an effective strategy? Could we have done more? Were we willing to take the risks that could have possibly stopped the war?

No matter which category is ours, let's not forget that in the United States we all live in the most affluent society in the history of the world, made possible in part by United States domination of the energy-rich Middle East and the resulting leverage over the world economy. Everywhere we look we see specks and logs. My sin in this matter may not be equal to the sins of president George Bush, former secretary of state Colin Powell, and general Tommy Franks, but how self-righteous should I feel because of that?

The consequences of these created sins are far more devastating than any injury we could cause individually, a fact difficult to face not just because of the enormity of the evil but because of the scale of the struggle necessary to change the systems from which the evil emerges. If we understand this sin as created and potential solutions as collective, then we realize the answer cannot come through religion alone nor through individual action; it must be political and pursued through organizing. We can't go off by ourselves to fix things, but instead must come together and face the enormous obstacles in the way of changing deeply entrenched systems.

We recognize that sin is inevitable, that we all have within us the capacity to violate our principles, and that experience tells us those violations will happen. But we also know that the nature of the social systems in which we live can encourage or discourage sin. White supremacy and patriarchy encourage white people and men to maximize their own narrow self-interest at the expense of nonwhite people and women. History also shows us how those with rights and privileges within imperial societies are, in this sense, sinners for their active participation in, or passive acceptance of, the brutality of empire. In the debates about white supremacy, patriarchy, and United States empire, there is no unified analysis nor call to action. But at least there is a debate, a recognition of the problem—people talk about the problems of racism, sexism, and militarism, and such conversations are possible in mainstream venues. While we must continue to call for justice on those questions, we also must recognize that our responsibility to speak in the prophetic voice about sin demands that we also be willing to call out the injustice of the predatory corporate capitalism that dominates not only this country but also the entire world.

THE SIN OF AND SINS IN CAPITALISM

Why might so many people in the United States dismiss as ludicrous the claim that our economic system is sinful? Perhaps because we are told it is the only way to live, relentlessly—typically by those who have much to gain from such a claim, most notably those in the business world and their apologists in the churches, schools, universities, mass media, and mainstream politics. Capitalism is not a choice, but rather simply *is*, like a state of nature. The claim can be even more overarching: Not *like a* state of nature, but *the* state of nature. In the past in the United States, when radicals and union organizers denounced capitalism, they were seen as a threat and typically met with violence and legal repression. Such resistance continues, but today contesting capitalism is like arguing against the air that we breathe. Arguing against capitalism, we're told, is simply crazy. When an eclectic mix of environmentalists, labor organizers, and leftists shut down the World Trade Organization meeting in Seattle in 1999 to protest the ravages of corporate globalization, *New York Times* columnist Thomas Friedman famously described them as "a Noah's ark of flat-earth advocates, protectionist trade unions and yuppies looking for their 1960's fix."[81] To an evangelical voice for global capitalism such as Friedman, an intellectually rigorous and morally principled opposition to capitalism is simply too strange to imagine in the brave new world of corporate domination that he trumpets in his column and books. The only explanation possible is that the protestors were stupid, self-interested, or self-indulgent.

Yet for many, something nags at us about such a claim; we are told "there is no alternative," and yet we experience that familiar feeling, "thank God it's Friday." It is true that capitalism is an incredibly productive system that has created a flood of goods and services unlike anything the world has ever seen, but is it really the only option? We're told we shouldn't even think about such things, but we can't help wondering: Is this really the "end of history," in the sense that theorists have used that

---

81 Thomas Friedman, "Senseless in Seattle," *New York Times*, December 1, 1999.

phrase, to signal the final victory of global capitalism administered by nations on the United States model?[82] Other theorists aren't so sure, claiming we now face a "return of history" that will require continued struggle to impose our superior vision for the world on the world.[83] But whatever phase of history we're in at the moment, it's difficult not to wonder whether the next phase is the actual end of the planet.

We wonder, we fret, and these thoughts nag at us for good reason: The predatory corporate capitalism that defines and dominates our lives will be our death if we don't escape it relatively soon. The call to speak prophetically about the sin of and sins in capitalism requires us not to pretend that minor modifications to the system can solve our problems and instead to speak of the system's basic injustice and unsustainability. It also demands that we say this not in jargon-ridden claims that tend to appeal only to sectarian, left groups but in straightforward language that can resonate with a wider audience. Here's my attempt at finding that language:

Capitalism is fundamentally inhuman, antidemocratic, and unsustainable. Capitalism has given those of us in the first world lots of stuff (though much of it of questionable value) in exchange for our souls, for our hope for progressive politics, and for the possibility of a decent future for children. Either we change or we die—spiritually, politically, literally.

---

82 Francis Fukuyama, *The End of History and the Last Man* (New York: Free Press, 1992).

83 Robert Kagan, *The Return of History and the End of Dreams* (New York: Knopf, 2008).

CAPITALISM IS INHUMAN

The theory behind contemporary capitalism explains that because we are greedy, self-interested animals, a viable economic system must reward greedy, self-interested behavior.

Are we greedy and self-interested? Of course. At least I am, sometimes. But we also just as obviously are capable of compassion and selflessness. We can act competitively and aggressively, but we also have the capacity to act out of solidarity and cooperation. In short, human nature is wide-ranging. In situations where compassion and solidarity are the norm, we tend to act that way. In situations where competitiveness and aggression are rewarded, most people tend toward such behavior.

Why is it that we must choose an economic system that undermines the most decent aspects of our nature and strengthens the cruelest? Because, we're told, that's just the way people are. What evidence is there of that? Look around, we're told, at how people behave. Everywhere we look, we see greed and the pursuit of self-interest. So the proof that these greedy, self-interested aspects of our nature are dominant is that, when forced into a system that rewards greed and self-interested behavior, people often act that way. Doesn't that seem just a bit circular? A bit perverse?

CAPITALISM IS ANTI-DEMOCRATIC

In the real world—not in the textbooks or fantasies of economics professors—capitalism has always been, and will always be, a wealth-concentrating system. If you concentrate wealth in a society, you concentrate power. I know of no historical example to the contrary.

For all the trappings of formal democracy in the contemporary United States, everyone understands that for the most part, the wealthy dictate the basic outlines of the public policies that are put into practice by elected officials. This is cogently explained by political scientist Thomas Ferguson's "investment theory of political parties," which identifies powerful investors rather than unorganized voters as the dominant force in campaigns and elections. Ferguson describes political parties in the United States as "blocs of major investors who coalesce to advance candidates representing their interests" and that "political parties dominated by large investors try to assemble the votes they need by making very limited appeals to particular segments of the potential electorate." There can be competition between these blocs, but "on all issues affecting the vital interests that major investors have in common, no party competition will take place."[84] Whatever we might call such a system, it's not democracy in any meaningful sense of the term.

People can and do resist the system's attempt to sideline them, and an occasional politician joins the fight, but such resistance takes extraordinary effort. Those who resist sometimes win victories, some of them inspiring, but to date concentrated wealth continues to dominate. If we define democracy as a system that gives ordinary people a meaningful way to participate in the formation of public policy, rather than just a role in ratifying decisions made by the powerful, then it's clear that capitalism and democracy are mutually exclusive.

To make this concrete: Our system is based on the principle that regular elections in which each person is entitled to one vote,

---

84 Thomas Ferguson, *Golden Rule: The Investment Theory of Party Competition and the Logic of Money-Driven Political Systems* (Chicago: University of Chicago Press, 1995), pp. 27–28.

along with protections for freedom of speech and association, guarantee political equality. When I go to the polls, I have one vote. When Bill Gates goes the polls, he has one vote. Bill and I both can speak freely and associate with others for political purposes. Therefore, as equal citizens in our democratic republic, Bill and I have equal opportunities for political power. Right?

CAPITALISM IS UNSUSTAINABLE

Capitalism is a system based on an assumption of continuing, unlimited growth. The last time I checked, this is a finite planet.

There are only two ways out of this problem. We can hold out hope that we might hop to a new planet soon, or we can embrace technological fundamentalism and believe that evermore complex technologies will allow us to transcend those physical limits here. Both those positions are equally delusional. Delusions may bring temporary comfort, but they don't solve problems; in fact, they tend to cause more problems, and in this world those problems seem to keep piling up.

Critics now compare capitalism to cancer.[85] The inhuman and antidemocratic features of capitalism mean that, like a cancer, the death system will eventually destroy the living host. Both the human communities and nonhuman living world that play host to capitalism will be destroyed by capitalism. It's in the nature of the system.

Capitalism is not, of course, the only unsustainable system that humans have devised, but it is the most obviously unsustainable

---

85 John McMurtry, *The Cancer Stage of Capitalism* (London: Pluto Press, 1999).

system, and it's the one in which we are stuck. It's the one that we are told is inevitable and natural, like the air we breathe. But if we were to face reality, we would conclude that Christianity—with its core commitments to love, equality, and stewardship—is incompatible with capitalism. Said more bluntly, capitalism is un-Christian, in theory and in practice.

AT HOME AND ABROAD, LET'S BE REALISTIC

In the first world, many of us struggle with alienation and fear. We often don't like the values of the world around us; we often don't like the people we've become; we often are afraid of the future and anxious about what's to come of us. But in the first world, most of us eat regularly. That's not the case everywhere. Let's focus not only on the conditions we face living in the most affluent country in the history of the world, but also put this in a global context. About 500 children in Africa die from poverty-related diseases, and the majority of those deaths could be averted with simple medicines or insecticide-treated nets. That's 500 children—not every year, or every month, or every week. That's not 500 children every day. In Africa, poverty-related diseases claim the lives of 500 children every hour.[86]

One of the common responses to such a condemnation of capitalism is, "Well, that may all be true, but we have to be realistic and do what's possible." By that logic, to be realistic is to accept a system that is inhuman, antidemocratic, and unsustainable. To be realistic, we are told, we must capitulate to a system

---

86 Kevin Watkins, "3 million reasons to act for Africa," *International Herald Tribune*, June 8, 2005. http://www.iht.com/articles/2005/06/07/news/edwatkins.php

that twists our souls, subordinates us to concentrated power, and will someday destroy the planet. To be realistic is to accept the death of the planet quietly, grateful for the toys that we are given to play with in the meantime.

What's truly realistic is organized resistance that is aware of the obstacles and the possibilities—setting sensible goals for the short term while always focusing on long-term threats, acting on the sense of urgency while pacing ourselves for the long haul. Most important is always speaking out, prophetically, with courage. Rejecting and resisting a predatory corporate capitalism is not crazy but is instead an eminently sane position. Holding onto our humanity is not crazy. Defending democracy is not crazy. And struggling for a sustainable future is not crazy. What is truly crazy is falling for the con that an inhuman, antidemocratic, and unsustainable system—one that leaves half the world's people in poverty—is all that there is, all that there ever can be, all that there ever will be. If that is true, then soon there will be nothing left, for anyone.

THE COSTS OF SPEAKING PROPHETICALLY

It may be crazy to accept such a fate quietly, but in fact most of the people in the United States do just that, which means that speaking prophetically is unlikely to make one popular. While everyone honors the prophets of the past, speaking in the prophetic voice in the present typically is not warmly received by all one's peers. A review of the prophets of the Old Testament offers some guidance on this.

First, remember that the prophets did not see themselves as having special status, but rather were ordinary people. When the king's priest confronted Amos for naming the injustice of his day, Amazi'ah called Amos a "seer" and commanded him to pack his bags and head to Judah and "never again prophesy at Bethel, for it is the king's sanctuary, and it is a temple of the kingdom." Amos rejected the label:

[14] Then Amos answered Amazi'ah, "I am no prophet, nor a prophet's son; but I am a herdsman, and a dresser of sycamore trees, [15] and the Lord took me from following the flock, and the Lord said to me, "Go, prophesy to my people Israel."

[AMOS 7:10-15]

Nor did the prophets seek out their calling. Jeremiah told God he did not know how to speak, claiming he was only a youth. God didn't buy the excuse:

[7] But the Lord said to me, "Do not say, 'I am only a youth'; for to all to whom I send you you shall go, and whatever I command you you shall speak. [8] Be not afraid of them, for I am with you to deliver you, says the Lord." [9] Then the Lord put forth his hand and touched my mouth; and the Lord said to me, "Behold, I have put my words in your mouth. [10] See, I have set you this day over nations and over kingdoms, to pluck up and to break down, to destroy and to overthrow, to build and to plant."

[JER. 1:7-10]

Nor was it typically much fun to fill the role of a prophet. On this, Jeremiah was blunt:

[9] Concerning the prophets: My heart is broken within me, all my bones shake; I am like a drunken man, like a man overcome by wine, because of the LORD and because of his holy words.

[JER. 23:9]

And, finally, the Old Testament reminds us that to speak prophetically involves more than just articulating abstract principles, which typically are relatively easy to proclaim. For example, these inspiring words from Micah are quoted often:

> [8] He has showed you what is good; and what does the Lord require of you but to do justice, and to love kindness, and to walk humbly with your God?
>
> [MIC. 6:8]

That is an eloquent way to summarize our core obligations, but at that level of generality, it is a statement that virtually all would endorse. Cite that verse and everyone will nod approvingly. But remember that Micah also was calling out the injustice around him and foretelling the inevitable consequences, never softening what he knew to be the truth:

> [12] Your rich men are full of violence; your inhabitants speak lies, and their tongue is deceitful in their mouth. [13] Therefore I have begun to smite you, making you desolate because of your sins. [14] You shall eat, but not be satisfied, and there shall be hunger in your inward parts; you shall put away, but not save, and what you save I will give to the sword. [15] You shall sow, but not reap; you shall tread olives, but not anoint yourselves with oil; you shall tread grapes, but not drink wine.
>
> [MIC. 6:12–15]

And:

> [2] The godly man has perished from the earth, and there is none upright among men; they all lie in wait for blood, and each hunts his brother with a net. [3] Their hands are upon

what is evil, to do it diligently; the prince and the judge ask for a bribe, and the great man utters the evil desire of his soul; thus they weave it together. [4] The best of them is like a brier, the most upright of them a thorn hedge. The day of their watchmen, of their punishment, has come; now their confusion is at hand.

[Mic. 7:2–4]

Before we can speak convincingly with such passion, we must achieve clarity in our own hearts, minds, and souls. To speak truthfully to others requires that we have first examined our own lives. When we call out the shortcomings of others, they typically ask us—and rightfully so—whether we have asked the same questions of ourselves. When we have asked and answered for ourselves, then we can find the courage to speak in that prophetic voice, knowing that we have confronted those questions and are willing to struggle with our own failures.

Our task is not to shine the light on others, but to shine the light from ourselves onto that which is wrong in the world. When we have been honest with ourselves, that light gains intensity and focus as it gathers within us. If we have turned away from a ruthless criticism of ourselves, that light will never reach the world and will illuminate nothing but our own limitations and fears.

THE PROPHETIC PATH TO LOVE

We live in a society that appears to be awash in political talk and religious activity. But in fact, our society is deeply depoliticized, full of political chatter on cable TV but lacking spaces in which we can have meaningful discussions about how to address problems that politicians often ignore. We live in a largely soulless culture; megachurches flourish, but many of us search for something beyond doctrine and dogma to help us answer questions that preachers often ignore. We live in a world in which politics are too often little more than public spectacle and religion is too easily cordoned off as a private matter.

In such a society, we don't need more politicians who avoid difficult problems that have no easy solutions. We don't need more preachers afraid of questions that go beyond the available answers. And we don't need a prophet—we need prophets, ordinary people who are willing to tap into the prophetic voice that is within us all.

To speak in that voice is not to claim exclusive insight or definitive knowledge; it is not to speak arrogantly. To speak in the prophetic voice is not to proclaim the truth self-righteously but to claim our rightful place in the collective struggle to understand the truth, which we seek in order to deepen our capacity to love. This we should never forget: We seek the prophetic voice within us to allow us to love more fully, something that Paul understood. When we call out injustice, when we find the courage to speak truths in a fallen world, it can be easy to be consumed by our anger and our grief, to lose track of that love. As we go forward to find the courage to speak prophetically, we should hold onto these words from Paul's first letter to the Corinthians:

[2] And if I have prophetic powers, and understand all mysteries and all knowledge, and if I have all faith, so as to remove mountains, but have not love, I am nothing.

[1 COR. 13:2]

Let us seek knowledge. We should pray that we stay strong in our faith in each other, that we help each other find the courage to speak prophetically. But, more than anything, let us remember to keep our hearts open so that we do not lose the capacity to love, always more, and always more authentically. That may be the defining quality of the prophetic; it is our authentic voice in which we speak the truth with love.

Authenticity is a tricky concept. It is a state or quality we often invoke, though we are not always clear about its meaning. The best definition of authenticity I've ever heard comes from one of the truly prophetic voices I have heard in my lifetime, my friend Abe Osheroff, who engaged joyfully in radical political activity until his death at the age of ninety-two.[87] Starting as a teenager in Depression-era New York helping evicted tenants, Abe was involved in progressive politics at every level—from fighting in the late 1930s for the Republic in the Spanish Civil War to community work in the civil rights movement in the United States, from neighborhood organizing against developers at home to the seemingly endless struggle to end United States wars around the world. Abe told me that in such political work, it is crucial to strive for authenticity, which he described simply and elegantly:

Authenticity comes when your thoughts, your words, and your deeds have some relation to each other. It comes when there's a real organic relationship between the way you think, the way you talk, and the way you act. You have to fight for authenticity all the time in this world, and if you don't fight for it you will get derailed. But when you have it, when you feel that surge of recognition—that I'm saying exactly what I'm thinking, and I'm

87 See the documentary film *Abe Osheroff: One foot in the grave the other still dancing*, dir. Nadeem Uddin, 2008.

ready to do something about it—well, that's an intellectual and emotional orgasm that makes sex look like nothing.[88]

When we speak prophetically we are not without fear but rather are willing to face our fears. In those authentically prophetic moments—when what we *think* matches what we *say* and matches what we *do*—we come closer to God.

---

88 Robert Jensen and Abe Osheroff, "On the Joys and Risks of Living in the Empire." http://www.thirdcoastactivist.org/osheroff.html

CONCLUSION

A New Communion

When I discuss these ideas with traditional Christians and with secular folks, I often get the same reaction: Why would I want to identify as a Christian, given that I have abandoned what are so often assumed to be beliefs central to the faith, such as the resurrection of Jesus as historical fact. I have been told by traditional Christians and secular people alike: Let's face it, we all know that's what a *real* Christian *really* believes. So why do I want to muddy the waters and complicate things with different definitions of terms, an alternative interpretation of the text, and an unorthodox profession of faith? The answer, of course, is that long before I stepped in, the waters were already quite muddy and always have been. I am not complicating Christianity, but instead Christianity—like all religious traditions—is perpetually self-complicating; it's in the nature of the theological endeavor. It's in the nature of being human. To repeat my observation from the beginning of the book:

Humans created religion; religion did not create humans.

This isn't heresy; it's common sense. Even if one believes that God is an entity, force, or being that created the world and us, there can be no doubt that we humans created religion, the vehicle for trying to understand any conception of God, and hence we are responsible for it. We're the ones who picked which pieces of the experiences and teachings of certain people should be central to understanding that God. We wrote the sacred texts. We make meaning from those texts. We choose how to act on those meanings. Even those who assert belief in a supernatural God have to understand that humans create the religion around that God.

In other words, there are no *real* Christians believing, thinking, and acting the way Christians *really* should. Instead, there are large numbers of real people in the world who find various kinds of inspiration in God, Jesus, and the Holy Spirit; in the traditions and texts of Christianity. These real people struggle to understand themselves, others, and humans' place in the world at least in part through that inspiration. The discussions and debates—the ideological wars that are taken so seriously that they sometimes lead to war—about how best to understand and live that struggle have been going on since the moment Christianity was born. Muslims, Jews, Hindus—and adherents of every other systematic attempt to understand what it means to seek God—could say the same thing. Religion would be a whole lot more useful if everyone acknowledged that.

This applies to everyone on all sides of every theological debate, including those I would most readily name as my allies. When fellow antiwar activists tell me that those who *really* want to follow Christ must be pacifists, I point out the simplistic nature of the claim. In the real world we face complex choices about our relationship to violence, and many Christians have sensible reasons to believe there are circumstances that justify the use of force, even deadly force. In advocating gay rights, I often say that one of my least favorite titles ever was a pro-gay book, *What the Bible Really Says about Homosexuality.*[89] When seeking guidance from the Bible on any serious issue, it's clear the text is far too complex—and sometimes internally contradictory—for anyone to make grandiose claims about what it *really* says about anything. A better title would have been *Some Ideas on What the Bible Says about Homosexuality.*

If I'm not a real Christian, then neither is anyone else. I claim the right to struggle with the ultimate questions within Christianity because those Christian concepts and stories belong to me, every bit as much as they belong to fundamentalists and moderates. Those concepts and stories are part of the culture into which I was born and they dominate the society that I want to help "bend toward justice."[90] If I had grown up in a predominantly Islamic country, I likely would be struggling to understand these things through Islam. And if that had been my place in the world, no doubt someone there would be telling me that I wasn't a real Muslim.

For many traditional Christians, this argument is not terribly compelling, and people often write to tell me that I simply don't understand what Christianity means. Sometimes they wish me luck in my search and offer to continue the correspondence if I think that would be helpful. Other times they conclude their correspondence about these matters, speaking as a kind of self-appointed faith police, with a demand that I stop using the term.

---

89 Daniel A. Helminiak, *What the Bible Really Says about Homosexuality* (San Francisco: Alamo Square Press, 1994).

90 I borrow the phrase from Martin Luther King Jr.: "Let us realize that the arc of the moral universe is long, but it bends toward justice." "Where Do We Go From Here?" (annual report to the Southern Christian Leadership Conference), August 16, 1967. http://www.stanford.edu/group/King/publications/speeches/Where_do_we_go_from_here.html

In my experience, the arrogance of those self-assured Christians matches the intensity of the arrogance of my secular correspondents, who chide me for wasting my time with superstitious traditions and advise me to focus on secular progressive politics where I belong. For those secular people, I return to the second part of my earlier claim:

Inanimate matter created life; life did not create inanimate matter.

This isn't debatable; it's the closest thing there is in science to fact. We humans should remember that for all our talk about being the most advanced form of life on the planet, our capacities pale in comparison with the creative force of nature. When humans give up the idea of God as an entity, force, or being that created the universe, it's crucial that we not start to believe we can slip quietly into God's place. A lot of secular people are quick to reject the notion of a Creator but just as quick to position humans in the role of the Supreme Being(s).

That's the supreme irony at the heart of the secular rejection of religion. Copernicus, Galileo, and modern science displaced earth (and, by implication, humans) from the center of the universe. We humans have had to come to terms with our cosmologically insignificant location in an incomprehensively expansive universe. Allegedly, we learned our place. But did we really? Think about the cavalier nature with which we destroy Creation to satisfy relatively trivial human desires—a good many of the accomplishments of modern science have been deployed in ways that suggest that we still see ourselves as being at the center of the universe. Maybe things don't revolve around us literally, but we seem to believe that they do in some larger philosophical sense, that our desires are at the center of it all. While the best scientists understand the need for humility and caution in the implementation of human discoveries, the culture of modern science and technology is notoriously arrogant, and it leads individuals and societies to take irrational risks. Hence the irony: The rationality in which science is rooted hasn't made us fundamentally more rational animals. Instead, it has propelled us to new manifestations of irrationality, leading us to the edge of degrading our ecosystem to such an extent that we will no longer be able to live. It's hard to get more irrational than that.

Humans are, as we've always been, creatures with rational and irrational aspects to our being. But the processes unleashed during the Age of Reason, the Scientific Revolution, and the Enlightenment—and fostered ever since by the secular worldview that dominates this period of human history—have accelerated the destruction of the planet in ways we are only starting to comprehend. Whatever damage to humans and the nonhuman world has resulted from the excesses of the religious and spiritual over the centuries—and that damage is extensive—it pales in comparison to the destruction caused by the excesses of the secular and scientific. The hubris of the modern human is sometimes breathtaking; surrounded by the big buildings and tiny electronic gadgets created through human cleverness, it's easy for us to believe that we are wise.

Experience seems to argue against that assumption, just as it argues against placing trust in religion specialists. Each side in the struggle—religious and secular—points to the failures of the other, to the myriad acts of wanton destruction carried out under the banner of Divine Inspiration and Human Reason. History counsels skepticism of both. Preachers tell us we can never know God, and then proceed to act as if they do. Scientists tell us that all knowledge is contingent and that we can never now anything for sure, and then proceed to act as if they know most everything. The track record of both is decidedly mixed.

GOD/GODS

The spiritual and the scientific are not mutually exclusive, but they often are seen as competing for primacy in our lives. When tough decisions need to be made, where should we look for guidance? This argument between the two camps must be reconciled, because if we stay deadlocked, the more destructive aspects of human nature are likely to continue unchecked, and there will be no hope of a decent future in the short run nor any kind of future in the long run. If we can escape the false alternatives—the religious versus the secular, spirituality versus science—then we can use our minds, hearts, souls, and strength to chart a new path. In that, our only hope is to recognize:

> There is no God, and more than ever we all need to serve the One True Gods.

The contradiction of the singular and plural—*one Gods*—is not meant as silly word play. In earlier sections of this book, I approached "God" as a descriptive term, arguing that we should understand it as a name people use for the mystery that is beyond our comprehension. That's fine as far as it goes, but it doesn't go far enough. If our theology is to be meaningful, it must reach beyond just naming our struggle and provide some guidance, offering not only a description of the human condition but help in figuring out how to live as well. This doesn't mean we must fall into the trap of thinking that centuries-old traditions and texts have definitive answers for today; we need guidance that draws on accumulated wisdom, not rules that short-circuit our own capacity to judge and act. We should explore our religious roots in the context of a wider history and philosophy, tested by what we can know through science, judged by the central criteria of justice and sustainability—and hope that with luck we can make our way forward.

If analysis leads us to understand God as a name for mystery—not as an entity, a force, or a being—then clearly God cannot be the object of worship in any traditional sense, nor can we expect God to answer our questions. We don't worship mystery or ask mystery to explain itself; instead we can only seek to deepen our understanding of it, a process in which we must use our minds, hearts, souls, and strength. The prescriptive aspect of this conception of God comes when we ask two key questions about our searching: First, on which aspects of the mystery should we focus, and, second, to serve whom? What questions should we ask, and who will benefit from the answers we find? This is where we can conceptualize the One True Gods.

Humans do seem to be innately curious; a lot of us like to figure out how things work. This curiosity doesn't form in a vacuum, of course; the impulse is channeled and shaped by social institutions, and we make choices about which facets of the world are most interesting to us. When we undertake serious efforts to understand the world, we are acting—implicitly or explicitly—on behalf of someone or something, whether it's our self-interest or the interest of some larger group or institution. That is, embedded in our choices is a conception of service and worship. Who are we explicitly serving and what are we implicitly worshipping when we struggle to try to understand this world and its mystery? The painful truth is that, most often in this society, we are worshipping money or power in the service of the corporation or the state. When the motive force behind so much of our inquiry is the desire to accumulate money and power, the questions we form about the world are intended to elicit information useful to corporations and governments. When we shape our inquiry to serve those masters, we are implicitly worshipping those gods.

Instead of the false gods of corporation and state, we should be serving community and communities, the One True Gods. We serve the One True Gods when our seeking process leads us to formulate questions aimed at generating answers that could benefit our community without harming (and helping when possible) the many other communities of the world. Our efforts should be focused at this most basic level, the communities where we are rooted, which we can truly know and love. At the same time, we should understand that our communities exist in connection with all other communities around the world. When we grasp this, we worship not money nor power but instead embrace life and love.

As I cautioned earlier, we must be careful about how we use the term "love." What does it mean to claim to love something or someone we will never know? Love can easily be drained of its meaning when tossed around so casually. While we love most fully in our community, that doesn't mean we can have no connection to, or feeling for, those in other communities. But that feeling is better described as empathy, not love. We are used to speaking of empathy in individual terms, the ability to understand how another person might be feeling. But that can, and should, be extended to the level of community. We need not pretend to love other persons to empathize with them; we have only to acknowledge their humanity, to recognize that they are, in moral terms, no different from us.

COMMUNITY/COMMUNITIES

The dual focus on the poles of our social existence—the relatively small number of people closest to us, and, at the same time, all the world—may seem odd at first. But it reflects the reality of our evolutionary history and the reality created by more recent history. We humans are, and always have been, tribal people. Throughout the vast majority of our history, humans lived in hunter-gatherer groups of probably no more than 150 people. This upper limit on human social networks, determined by our cognitive capacity, has been called "Dunbar's number" (after anthropologist Robin Dunbar)—the number of individuals with whom any one of us can maintain stable relationships.[91]

There have been huge changes in social organization in the 10,000 years since humans have become agricultural, intensified in the few centuries dominated by the nation-state and the two centuries of the industrial revolution. However, it was that hunter-gatherer history, lived in small-scale social organization, that shaped us into the kind of animal we are. Because we are self-conscious beings, we should hesitate to say that human behavior is ever purely "natural"—that is, dictated solely by processes outside our control—unless we want to abandon any notion of free will. Yet we can't ignore that band or tribe affiliation was the organizational norm for at least 95 percent of our species' evolutionary history.

While first world folks are fond of labeling the so-called

---

91 See Robin Dunbar, *The Human Story* (London: Faber and Faber, 2004). For a video summary, see Robin I.M. Dunbar, "Mind the Gap: Why Humans Aren't Just Great Apes," presentation to Gustavus Adolphus College Nobel Conference XLIV, October 7–8, 2008, St. Peter, Minnesota. http://gustavus. edu/events/nobelconference/2008/dunbar-lecture.php

"primitive" people around the world as tribal, we are all tribal in our basic nature, no matter what kind of political organization we live in today. That's why large institutions create ways for people to forge identities as a smaller scale. For example, at my university, incoming students can join a "freshman interest group" of about twenty students in their specific college to help them cope with living in a population of nearly 50,000 students. While part of the draw of megachurches is the large services on Sunday, what anchors the churches' core members are the many small groups based on common interests that meet throughout the week for prayer and fellowship.[92]

Wes Jackson, who has advocated for changes in industrial agriculture modeled on lessons from natural ecosystems, makes a similar point about seeking guidance for shaping society. If we look to nature for insight about sustainable structures for human living, our pre-agricultural evolutionary history becomes a guide for understanding how to deal with basic needs. For Jackson, that points to community, which he describes as

> civilization's upscaling of the gathering-hunting tribe. Why community works has at least as much to do with the way nature shaped us as with the way agriculture and culture have shaped us.[93]

This is not a plea to go back in time but an argument for paying attention to our history as we go forward. With more than 6.5 billion people on the planet, obviously we couldn't go back to hunting and gathering even if we wanted to. With the overwhelming injustice produced by 500 years of an imperialism

---

92 Malcolm Gladwell, "The Cellular Church," *New Yorker,* September 12, 2005.

93 Jackson, *Becoming Native to this Place,* pp. 52–53.

that radiated most intensely from Europe and the United States, we can't ignore the moral obligations we have at the global level. We are a species most fully attuned to the local and the particular, but history demands that we contend with our existence on a planetary level as well.

There's no guarantee we can pull that off; it's unclear whether, as a species, we have the intellectual resources and moral capacity to create a sustainable future. But if we are to have any hope, our struggle to understand the mystery of this world—our quest to know God—must focus on those two levels: our community and all communities. That means when we ask how we are to use our minds, hearts, souls, and strength to engage the mystery—that is, when we ask what we are to worship and serve—the answer is found at those two levels: the most local and particular, the community in which we live and love; and the most universal and abstract, the worldwide network of communities with which we must empathize so that we can coexist.

We are both particular and universal. We live in the world in a specific place, one of many different places. We live in a community that is one of millions of communities. The task is to seek the mystery through engagement with our local communities, remembering that our foundational sense of connection to the world comes through local connections—it is those local connections that remind us those other communities exist around us. Hence, there is One True Gods of community and communities.

And there are, of course, many false gods: the institutions created beyond the level of community, whose basic function is almost always to control those communities, aggrandizing the power of some group of elites. Beyond our communities are the bureaucratic institutions of church, corporation, and nation-state. These are false gods, not because nothing good ever happens within them but because when we submit to the interests of these institutions—which means the interests of the relatively small number of people who direct them—ordinary people within communities and the nonhuman world tend to suffer. These institutions of the false gods are not rooted in our evolutionary history, nor do they embody universal principles. They are vehicles for power-over, and hence are inherently untrustworthy. As Jackson has pointed out, if these institutions were consistent with our evolutionary history, they wouldn't need bureaucracies to define, control, and enforce rules.

So this conception of One True Gods does not ask us to pretend that we can love all the people and places of the world equally. Instead, it reminds us that the core of our humanity is our place in community and that any real community is held together by love. Because our community exists in a world among others, that love can survive and we can flourish only when we can empathize with those whom we don't love, with a moral understanding that those in the other communities are just like us. For all people—no matter where or how they live—making good on our humanity must mean taking care of our own and reaching out beyond our community to others when we can.

But more is demanded of those of us who are living the "good life" as a direct result of a violent imperial history—that is, the vast majority of us living in the contemporary United States. If we are serious about our stated principles and the faith we claim to hold, we are obligated to correct those past injustices and work against the ongoing evils perpetrated by our nation-state and our corporations, which deepen the injustice. That is no small task, especially when the systems we have an obligation to undermine are the very same ones that produce the affluence that leads so many people to turn away from this call.

My initial interest in returning to Christianity was motivated by the difficult task of organizing for progressive politics in such a country. Given my status on top of the privilege pile—a white man in a white-supremacist patriarchal culture, living a relatively comfortable middle-class existence in a global economic system dominated by the nation of which I am a citizen—the primary focus of my organizing has been enlisting people like me to work against our own short-term material self-interest. That is difficult in a culture that focuses our attention on our individual success defined in material terms and rewards us for playing that game.

Self-identified Christians end up on all sides of these issues. While some would agree with my assessment, many others would argue strenuously that the United States is the fullest embodiment of Christian values and that corporate capitalism is the essence of freedom. This wide variation in interpreting traditions and texts means that "Christian" is a term that carries no information. When people whom I do not know tell me they are Christians, there is nothing I can know for sure about those people—I can't make any prediction about their theology or politics. The same could be said for the terms "Jew," "Muslim," and "Hindu." In a world of so many divergent theologies within traditions, there is, in fact, no such thing as Christianity, but merely competing visions of Christianity.

No matter what one's religious orientation, the struggle to define what it means to be Christian is an important one in the United States and by virtue of United States power, an important one in the world. My interest in this may have been purely political at first, but it quickly went further, as I realized that posing this question was not only relevant for my political work but also a way for me to reflect on—not merely parrot answers to—fundamental questions that we all must face.

WHAT IS AT THE CORE OF CHRISTIANITY?

In Christianity, as in any organized religion, there are major doctrinal disputes within the tradition as well as battles for primacy with other traditions. Two of the most crucial questions for Christians to consider are, first:

Does Christianity name *a process of seeking* or is it defined by *the declaration of belief?*

And second:

Are we to understand God and Jesus as being *with us but outside of us* or *with us, within us?*

Historian Elaine Pagels has shown that there were Christians in the early history of the faith who would have answered "seeking" and "within us" to those questions but whose perspective was excluded as the church imposed a different view as orthodoxy.[94] She argues that the Gospel of John, which was written after the other three New Testament gospels, was probably produced to support the emerging orthodoxy of "declaration of belief" and "outside of us," which Christians have lived with ever since. John's text ended up in the New Testament and Thomas's was labeled heresy, lost to the world until rediscovered in 1945 in Egypt, one of the famous Nag Hammadi texts.[95]

This history suggests that my preferred answers to those questions have a historical antecedent in the Thomas Christians, but

---

94 Elaine Pagels, *Beyond Belief: The Secret Gospel of Thomas* (New York: Random House, 2003).

95 The Nag Hammadi Library, including the Gospel of Thomas, is online. http://www.gnosis.org/naghamm/nhl.html

that hardly makes my interpretation definitive. We learn from the past, but the past does not necessarily reveal the truth. Ancient texts remind us that throughout history people have struggled with the same questions we do, but those texts don't relieve us of our need to answer for ourselves. Each generation, in the context of its historical moment, has to pursue its solutions, which will always be contingent and conditional.

Part of the difficulty of all this is attempting to establish a morally acceptable way of life despite our intellectual limits. As we mature, individually and collectively, we should become aware of how little we can understand about the world, and yet at the same time we should feel compelled to act for the sake of justice and sustainability. As the problems we face in that central task become evermore complex, we need more knowledge than we can acquire. If we want to eliminate poverty, for example, exactly how do we in the United States contribute to that project while living in a militarized hypernationalist state dominated by predatory capitalist corporations? If we want to reverse global warming to make it possible to imagine future generations living decent lives on the planet, how do we do that in a world with an oil-based infrastructure feeding delirious hyperconsumption? There always are steps we can take, but there is no way to do more than sketch tentative answers to such questions—redefining a good life, learning to live with less, moving away from capitalism, and finding a level of political organization that can truly operate democratically.

In these endeavors, we have to face that we know far less than we need to know. And at the same time, we must dramatically intensify our activities even though we don't know enough. In other words, we must be humble enough to admit how much we don't know while at the same time finding new courage to take far greater risks in acting on this woefully imperfect knowledge. For me, Christianity—or any other religion—can help in this struggle only if we understand theology as a process of seeking that can remain dynamic and open, rather than a declaration of beliefs that are static and closed. For me, Christianity—or any other religion—can be the basis for courage only if we understand God as being within us all, giving us a source of power-with, rather than outside of us, opening up the inevitable abuses of power-over.

My answers are the result of a long and painful process in my mind, what I feel when I try to still myself and know what is in my heart, what settles into my soul when I feel my mind and heart truly integrated, and what give me the strength I need to live with hope. My answer is to love the mystery of it all, in the company of others on a similar path. A passage from the once-heretical Gospel of Thomas expresses much of this for me:

> Jesus said: "If you bring forth what is within you, what you bring forth will save you. If you do not bring forth what is within you, what you do not bring forth will destroy you."[96]

What we have within us, together, is enough. I owe it not only to myself but others to bring forth what is within me. We should remember that the Thomas Christians were committed not just to the personal exploration of what it meant to be Christian, but to a communal enterprise of mutual care and compassion. In a crucial New Testament passage describing the early Christians—one that is usually conveniently overlooked because it so clearly points out the nature of the false gods worshipped in the contemporary United States—we are reminded of what "communal" meant to those people:

---

96 Thomas: 70, as translated by George MacRae and quoted in Pagels, *Beyond Belief*, p. 32.

[44] And all who believed were together and had all things in common; [45] and they sold their possessions and goods and distributed them to all, as any had need. [46] And day by day, attending the temple together and breaking bread in their homes, they partook of food with glad and generous hearts, [47] praising God and having favor with all the people. And the Lord added to their number day by day those who were being saved.

[ACTS 2:44–47]

Being saved came not merely through profession of belief but through a way of living. This reminder of the possibility of a deeper communal living than most of us experience today helps illuminate another problem in progressive politics. In my organizing efforts, I often talked with people who shared my analysis of an issue, such as the injustice of the murderous economic embargo on Iraq in the 1990s or the routine denial of workers' rights in corporate capitalism. But when I asked them to join in collective action to address the problem, many people would say, "I can't stand meetings," or, "I hate belonging to groups."

Most of us have sat through meetings that left us agitated and annoyed at others (I'm thinking here of university faculty meetings as the paradigm case), just as we have been in groups where we felt alienated and unfulfilled (which describes high school for many). But rather than reject all meetings or groups, it would be more accurate to say, "I can't stand meetings in which people don't understand how to work together," or, "I hate belonging to groups that exacerbate differences rather than emphasize commonalities." In other words, unless one is a genuine misanthrope, we don't dislike being with people to achieve common aims, nor are we generally antisocial. We reject those experiences when the systems and structures in which we live make it impossible to experience meaningful communal connection. We run away from such experiences when being bound to others feels suffocating rather than invigorating.

Human beings who live communally do not magically become mutually agreeable at all times, nor does a common religious faith erase the inevitable differences in temperament that can cause conflict. While we cannot claim that all the ways we annoy one another are all the product of the perverse hierarchy of corporations or of political structures, certainly the degree to which we annoy each other is greatly affected by the nature of the institutions in which we work and live and their larger cultural context. In a hyperindividualized, materialistic culture based on hierarchy, it's not surprising that so many avoid meetings and groups.

We need not romanticize other forms of organization to begin the search for new directions. For example, when I have taught Wendell Berry's novel *Jayber Crow*[97] in my first-year seminar, one of the main points of discussion is Berry's nuanced discussion of community. The book is one in a series of novels and short stories that explores the fictional town of Port William, Kentucky, over generations. Berry repeatedly refers to "the Port William membership," emphasizing that this is not just a collection of people living in and around a town, but a community in a deeper sense. Berry refuses to paint an idyllic picture of rural small-town life. His characters share the flaws and frailties to be found in any group; there are both admirable and unpleasant characters running throughout the ongoing story of Port William. But until that community is destroyed by the greed and power-seeking of forces that come largely from outside, usually through the corporation and/or the nation-state, the community endures. Port William works.

---

97 Wendell Berry, *Jayber Crow* (Washington, DC: Counterpoint, 2001).

We are reminded by sources such as the Book of Acts and Berry that real community does not depend on some exotic formula, and it can exist under varied realistic conditions. The Port William membership lived in a world based on private property and profit, not on the communal ownership of the early Christians, but the destructive forces of capitalism were held in check for some time. No single community is free of the sins of the greater culture; Berry is not hesitant, for example, to mark the racism that lives in a predominantly white community. It is the success within such struggles, not the illusion of a community without struggles, from which we can take heart.

We can look to the past to think about what must be in the future. A new sense of the communal is needed to overcome the barriers that keep people from acting on what they feel and believe, and one of the sources of that communal spirit can be Christianity. Unfortunately, in many Christian churches the sense of community is largely absent. No matter what the nature of people's profession of faith in God, the false gods of the culture can shape our lives and outlooks. In a world where the term "communion" means nothing more to many people than a church ritual that they plod through by rote, we need a New Communion if Christianity is to be a meaningful force for justice and sustainability.

A NEW COMMUNION

It is commonplace to hear people suggest that small communities work only when people have no choice, when they have to trust and rely on each other because of some threatening condition in the world, such as scarcity. Hunting-gathering tribes worked because people had to cooperate to survive, I've been told, or small towns worked when the limits of transportation and communication technology meant people were stuck with each other. These comments typically are made by people living in a hyper-individualized consumer culture, often with what appears to be little self-reflection on how contemporary culture might affect their perceptions of all this. But let's say, for the sake of argument, that such assertions are correct: We humans come together in community only in situations when we have to, and we would otherwise prefer to operate as the greedy self-interested beings that capitalism preaches we really are.

If it's true that these kinds of needs drive community, then never have we needed community more than we do now. The only way to imagine reversing the potentially terminal moral and ecological damage is by stepping away from the systems that produce the destruction and imagining a just and sustainable life in meaningful community.

This is not an attempt to erase individuality (in the sense of the many differences among people), but instead a rejection of individualism (in the sense of a philosophy that places the desires of individuals ahead of the greater good of the community).[98] This is not an attempt to recreate some mythical golden age of harmony and love. To repeat: We humans, under any circumstances, are likely to annoy each other at times. The question is, how do we create the social systems, structures, and stories that help us look past those differences to what we have in common?

Both the Latin (*communio*) and the Greek (*koinonia*) roots of our word "communion" invoke notions of sharing within a fellowship. Sharing is an ongoing process made real not by statements of belief but by many small acts of cooperation and connection.

---

98 I borrow this formulation from Marilyn A. Friedman, "Individuality without Individualism," *Hypatia* 3:2 (Summer 1988): 131–137.

Fellowship trains our attention not on a God in the sky but on ourselves and each other. To determine whether one should join with another in community, we could ask, as many do, "Do we both believe the same claims about a God outside of us?" But we would be better served by asking, "Do we both struggle to find within ourselves the light of God in connection with others?" The first question focuses us on doctrines and dogma that end up being of little consequence. The second question need not ignore doctrinal differences but instead highlights what can unite us.

The strongest bonds of community occur in places we know and among people we know. That does not mean we can connect only with people who look or think exactly like us. In my experience, those bonds have been created across differences in age, race, gender, culture, and religion when people were working toward common goals. In all of those connections that have made it possible for me to work with others in progressive politics, there was a core commitment to justice and sustainability, and we had the time and space to get to know one another. Most of the political groups in which those connections were formed have not survived, which is hardly surprising; in an affluent and mobile culture, it's all too easy for us to go our separate ways when working in groups becomes difficult. But it is in those groups that I have seen what is possible, and from those groups I have formed networks of friends and allies who remain connected through political work and fellowship. Such friendship networks are not a community, but they remind us of what is possible.

The persistence of these networks based on personal relationships also suggests that we are most likely to succeed if we begin the process of building community not by trying immediately to gather a community as large as 150 people together. Given the reality of the lives many of us lead, such a strategy would be difficult unless one wanted to pander to the worst instincts of the dominant culture by creating a setting for self-gratification (the strategy of many successful churches) rather than real community. Instead, we'd be wise to start much smaller, in circles of like-minded people willing to commit to each other over time in a specific place.

Although there is much talk of the value of electronic networking, I do not believe online connections can form the basis of the community-building required in the future. People have told me they feel as close, or even closer, to those whom they "know" online than to people around them in physical space, which I don't doubt. But I take that as a distressing indicator, not a hopeful one; it is a reminder of just how impoverished our day-to-day connections to others in our lives can be, either because of the effects of oppressive systems (such as lesbian and gay youth who are isolated in hostile communities) or affluence (such as suburban residents whose lives revolve around electronic entertainment and communication). We are not free-floating minds, but embodied creatures, and I cannot imagine how computer-mediated communication can replace direct human interaction, any more than did the printing press, telephone, or any other communication technology. The work of building a just and sustainable world is going to be primarily work in the world on the ground, not in a virtual world online. Digital technologies can be helpful as channels for communication in some projects, but nothing I see in their current use (or can imagine in some future use) suggests they can create the kind of place-bound community that I think will be necessary in the future. Place matters. As Berry has said, "You can't know who you are if you don't know where you are."

If one wanted to take the disciples as a model, without the

idea of a messianic leader, we could form circles of twelve. Not a dozen people looking to a prophet, but a dozen people willing to speak in the prophetic voice, first to each other and then to the larger world.

How one circle might link to others is not clear, but it is unnecessary to try to predict this development. Various models for confederation exist, and no doubt the varying conditions from place to place will require different strategies at different historical moments.

Global realities no longer allow us to pretend. We live amidst cascading crises that demand not further attempts at industrial heroism to solve discrete problems, but a recognition that the problem is in the systems and structures we have created. The problem is rooted in the kind of humans we have become in a power-over world. The only hope is to recognize there are no solutions within these power-over systems and to begin the painful work of imagining a new way, with no guarantee of success. I have no blueprint for that work, nor does anyone else. The broad outlines of how we will live—not how we *may*, but how we *must* and *will* live—in a world not subsidized by easily accessible fossil fuels are clear: a dramatic reduction in energy use and consumption more generally; a radical restructuring of transportation, with the end of easy air and car travel; a transformation of agriculture toward the seasonal and local, almost entirely sun-powered. Equally clear is that we in the first world must stop the ongoing practice of extracting wealth from the third world and begin to reverse that flow, in recognition that much of our wealth was extracted from there and that the conditions there, no matter what the economic history, demand it.

Technological fundamentalists dream of illusory high-technology and high-energy solutions that they imagine will allow us to continue to consume, while economic and national fundamentalists tell us we owe nothing to the third world other than to encourage them to dream of one day becoming consumers, too. This is our ironic state of existence: Though drastic action is more necessary than ever, the last gasps of those three dying fundamentalisms are digging in to try to ignore reality and abandon moral obligations. Those projects are doomed to fail.

Religious fundamentalists are a bit of a wild card. For example, many Christian fundamentalists recognize that the current United States culture, saturated with images of commodified sexuality, is a death trap. Yet rather than identify the dual problems of patriarchy and capitalism at the root of that problem, they hold tightly to patriarchy and refuse to condemn capitalism, preferring to scapegoat feminists, lesbians, and gays. On global warming, the Evangelical Climate Initiative takes an important first step in acknowledging that there is "overwhelming evidence that human activity is a major cause, and we know that the impacts of climate change would be hardest on the poor and vulnerable, and on future generations."[99] But the statement makes no mention of the systemic changes that are necessary to address the issue in a serious manner, instead preferring to recycle empty warnings against "unnecessary government regulations" and promote fantasies that the "free market" will be able to solve the problem.[100] Many people have a visceral sense that there is something dramatically wrong in our world, but too often the fear produced by that sense leads to tragically flawed analyses.

Can we see that this fundamentalist theology takes us in

99 Evangelical Climate Initiative, "Christians and Climate." http://www.christiansandclimate.org/

100 Evangelical Climate Initiative, "Principles for Federal Policy on Climate Change." http://christiansandclimate.org/pubs/PrinciplesforFederalPolicyonClimateChange.pdf

the wrong direction, yet also reject a moderate theology that typically leaves us treading water? Can we forge a truly radical theology that can be central to this transformation? That is not a matter for prediction, but for action. It is possible if we create a New Communion, rejecting the false gods that dominate our lives today. That New Communion is the seed of the dream of a new world that might someday come alive. It is hope piled upon hope, with no guarantee. Such hope is difficult to maintain, which is why, in addition to thinking through these things at abstract levels, we have to search our everyday experience for "the authentic underpinnings of hope."[101]

COMMUNION AND THE SACRAMENTAL SALAD

Holy communion, the symbolic sharing of wine and bread, is an important practice in many Christians' experience of church. Each time my pastor, Jim Rigby, conducts that service at St. Andrew's, he reminds us that this is not a supernatural ritual in which wine becomes blood and bread becomes body. Rather it is a coming together to remember who we are and what we struggle to be. That act of marking our collective existence need not be confined to church in a formalized procedure; we can look for the same experience in our everyday lives.

For me, the most important communion service has taken place outside of church, led not by a minister but by a friend who is part of no religious tradition. James Koplin, who has been a teacher, organizer, and community volunteer throughout his life, also is a first-rate gardener. All those experiences have

---

101 Wendell Berry, "Conservation and Local Economy," in *Sex, Economy, Freedom & Community* (New York: Pantheon, 1993), p. 11.

played a part in how he has come to understand and analyze the world, how he faces honestly the reality of the decline that leaves him every day "in a state of profound grief," an acknowledgment of the pain of the world and the severity of the crises.

Yet at the same time I know of no one who so thoroughly experiences joy in everyday life, especially the acts of growing, preparing, and sharing food. Though Jim claims no religious identification, he may be the most devout Christian I know, not only in the ways he contributes to the world but in his habits as well. One of these is what we friends refer to as Koplin's "sacramental salad," which is the final phase of virtually every dinner at his house. The recipe is simple: lettuce, onions, olive oil, mustard, and red wine vinegar, with a few seasonings, lightly applied, and a bit of blue cheese. In the nearly twenty years I have known Jim, he has always used the same glass bowl and stainless steel utensils to prepare the salad, always with the same sequence of steps. He wears the same blue-and-white-striped apron around the kitchen. We have a routine for eating it, in which we each take a substantial portion the first time around and then split what is left in a second round. The final act is to use bread or tortillas to absorb whatever oil remains in the bowl.

Our meals, culminating with that sacrament, mark our communion. When others join us, the process is modified to welcome them. When Jim eats with others, they have their own version of it, similar in most ways but unique to them. When there is lettuce coming from Jim's garden in summer, the salad has special meaning. Even in winter when all the ingredients may be store-bought, the salad carries some essence of Jim. Those of us who have had Jim's salad try to replicate it in our own kitchens, but I can never get it quite right; Jim has a touch with this particular sacrament that can't be taught. Eventually, we all learn to stop trying to make Jim's salad and make our own, recognizing that it is not the food but the space created by the ritual that is most important.

We all have routines in our daily lives, and some of those routines can become rituals. No doubt others have their own versions of communion out of church, which we so desperately need to help each other through life. Some of the most important conversations I have had with Jim, which are some of the most important in my life, have come over that salad bowl. Not all have been happy conversations, for that space created allows us not only to feel the joy but also the grief.

We live in a culture that offers lots of cheap pleasures and cheap ways to reduce pain. Television programs amuse us while the advertisements peddle myriad ways to numb us. But again, as Berry reminds us, we live on "the human estate of grief and joy." There is much pleasure in the experience of joy, but joy can't be purchased. There is much pain when we grieve, but grief shouldn't be feared. The false gods promise to provide us with pleasure and relieve our pain. A more authentic faith is about the struggle to embrace our grief and deepen our joy. What we seek in communion is not personal pleasure but a collective sense of joy. In communion we do not seek to numb pain but rather to accept grief.

Each day that I go forward I learn a little bit more about the nature of unnecessary human suffering and the dire condition of the nonhuman world. Each day I have a better understanding of the deeply entrenched systems of power that create this suffering and threaten all of life. Each day I wake up a little more scared about the future, with a slightly deeper sense of grief. And each day I also wake up aware that there is more joy in the world than I ever knew.

In other words, each day I wake up and struggle to choose to live consciously on that human estate, with that grief and joy. In a world in which so many false gods offer a path to cheap pleasure and escape from pain, this struggle is always difficult. But it is worth it. When deciding which path to go down, which gate to enter, we should remember where false gods lead us.

THE NARROW GATE TO LIFE

In the Sermon on the Mount, Jesus was clear about our choices:

> [13] Enter by the narrow gate; for the gate is wide and the way is easy that leads to destruction, and those who enter by it are many. [14] For the gate is narrow and the way is hard that leads to life, and those who find it are few.
>
> [MATT. 7:13–14]

In the contemporary United States, the corporation and the nation-state make it easy to enter through their gates, which are open wide and entice us with promises of immediate gratification, in both material and ideological terms. We can shop till we drop and believe we live in the greatest nation on earth, remaining willfully ignorant about the consequences of our attempts to dominate the world. Today many people—including many who would identify as devout Christians—enter through those gates without hesitation, precisely because it is so easy. Those who want to choose life must do the work not only of organizing to help others and change these systems, but also of publicly proclaiming our choice of the narrow gate. Rather than hiding among those we trust, we have to reach out, prophetically, and risk the inevitable accusations of heresy.

While we should not pretend that way to life is easy, we also must remind people that no one finds that path alone. As is often the case, one finds echoes of the wisdom of religious texts in secular art and political philosophy. In "Bread and Circuses," a contemporary song about the hypocrisy of so much organized religion, Billy Bragg and Natalie Merchant remind us: "The gates of hell stand open wide, but the path of glory you walk single file."

Again, the seductive choice, through the wide-open gate, is the one that doesn't challenge the false gods, but that is the way to hell. In this picture, not only do we enter through the narrow gate but then must walk the path of glory single file, with no one by our side. That does not mean we are alone. When we walk together in single file, there is someone ahead of us who can reach back to help us if we stumble, and we are there to reach back to another. When we struggle, as we always will, we can take comfort in trusting that we can reach out for that hand of another, and take responsibility for those who will need our hand.

And, of course, not every moment of life is spent in solitude, choosing narrow gates and narrow paths. There are many moments when we stop and gather together to remind ourselves why we choose what is hard. These are moments of the sacred, which we sometimes turn into ritual, sacraments that happen not only at the altar with the Eucharist but also around a dinner table. These are moments of communion, when we come together in church or on picket lines, to find our freedom in our obligations to each other. The authentic underpinnings of hope exist.

These are moments of grief and joy, the moments when we glimpse what it means to be human. I find them not by looking toward a God in heaven but to the mystery inside myself and in my community, connected forever to the mystery of the other and the communities of the world.

To find these moments in this world, so saturated with injustice and teetering on the edge of collapse, takes all my mind, heart, soul, and strength.

To find all this, and to dream of more, takes faith.

Not a naïve and selfish faith that if we endure long enough things will turn out just fine.

Not a naïve and selfish faith that even if things don't work out on earth, there is another realm in which we will receive our reward.

Instead, we need a much deeper faith, one that accepts the often painful struggle with mystery that is inevitable if we are to live truly alive on the human estate of grief and joy.

Faith comes when we understand that the reward of that struggle is not only the joy but also the grief.

In my mind, that is what I feel it means to be human.

In my heart, that is what I think it means to be human.

In my soul, I pray for the strength to be human.